D1617514

WITHDRAWN

HOW *Music*
EXPRESSES *Ideas*

Sidney Finkelstein

INTERNATIONAL PUBLISHERS, NEW YORK

First printing, February, 1952
Second printing, September, 1952

CONTENTS

1. *Music and Human Images*

THERE ARE MANY MORE BOOKS to be found today on the pleasures of music than on its meanings. Most listeners to music in the United States today will say that they are seeking only pleasure. Certainly if music did not give pleasure, it would have no reason for existence as an art; the question is not that of the pleasures of music as against its meanings, but whether people can create a worthwhile music if to them it is a meaningless art.

To understand the meanings of music does not detract from its pleasures, but adds to them. There are two kinds of pleasure that art gives. One is the ten-times familiar experience, the soothing of the senses as a refuge from the troubles of life. The other is the excitement of awakening the mind through the senses to some aspect of the real world and of human life and thought that had previously been unknown or a mystery. It is the latter pleasure, the pleasure of learning, which is the fundamental one that great art provides in its own time. It is a special kind of learning—that which brings about a feeling of growth in the beholder, with a consciousness of heightened powers.

Only if we understand the meanings of music, and see that the creation of great music requires conscious thinking not only about musical techniques but about people in society, can we stimulate and bring into being music which is nearer to our desires and needs.

Music, technically speaking, is an art of sounds organized in relationships of pitch and rhythm. It is a development of the human voice, of the ear, and of skills in fashioning musical instruments which enable sounds to be organized with greater richness and complexity, thus developing further the voice and ear. Music, however, could not have been developed simply out of curiosity among human beings as to how sounds could be manipulated. It has been from its very beginning an emotional activity of human beings, a way of giving these emotions outer form. Something of its power may be seen when we imagine

5

even ordinary speech without inflections, accents, and intonations, which are the "music" of words. The essential power of spoken language as a medium of thought lies in its word meanings and grammar. The "music" of speech, however, adds the essential human quality, giving to these thoughts the added tone of emotion that in real life accompanies every human action, sensation, and idea.

There is nothing mysterious about emotions. They are aroused by everything a person perceives and does, by every relationship between one person and his fellow human beings. They are a sign of the fact that every perception and action has some role to play in the life, growth, and development of the human being. The feeling of beauty, so central to music, is the joy that accompanies the leap in knowledge, the recognition of a common bond among human beings. It arises from the transformation of a relationship to nature or other human beings that had seemed harmful or destructive into one that becomes fruitful, permitting the human being to live and grow more freely. Works of music contain, at their core, human images, typical human actions and relationships. It is the presence of these human images that enables music to arouse emotions. The history of music is, first of all, the history of the development of human images in sound, and of the techniques and skills with voice, fingers, body, and musical instruments that enable these images to be created with increasing richness. This development is always social, for it is the product of innumerable acts and discoveries, each adding to the other, and each tested by its meaning to a community of people.

Works of music also convey ideas. Ideas are the understanding of the relationship among things and people, generalizations which are the product of innumerable human actions and discoveries, insights into the deeper laws underlying the movement of nature and society. Ideas are not emotions. However, ideas transform the real life of human beings, and so change their emotional life.

Musical works embody the thoughts of the composer, which are seen in their product, in the organization of human imagery and emotional life, real yet generalized, taken from life and conveyed in his music. To understand the meanings of works of music we have to ask how the people lived; what were the divisions between those who labored and those who owned the means of production; what social class did the music serve; what were its world views, its views of human beings, nature, and society. It is possible to write a history of music which describes only the techniques and forms, and the superficial color of the times which produced them. Such a description, however, ignoring the social activities and thinking out of which the music sprang, deprives the music of meaning and then claims that it is meaningless. To understand music, it is necessary to put it back into the context of the real life that created it.

To see works of music historically, and as a product of class society, is not to negate their permanent worth. To the extent that works of music are realistic, or in other words reflect human life faithfully, and develop the techniques for the fuller depiction of human life, they are a permanent addition to the cultural heritage. Yet these works are at the same time dated. For all their power, they are inadequate to satisfy fully the cultural needs of later times, for life has raised and mastered new problems and developed new ideas. And so new works must always be created, and new problems of technique and form must be raised, using the past heritage. And works of the past are by no means equal in their lasting power. The history of music is one of great advances in realism, and also of countless examples of formalism, the imposition of manacles and a blind use of tradition upon the ability of human beings to explore and master the world they live in.

This book is a study of the development of the meaning of music. It is not a history, but it must necessarily approach the subject historically, giving some idea of the way in which the art has taken on new experiences, problems, and ideas.

It deals, but for some discussion of origins, with the European music of the past five hundred years and with the problems of music in the United States today. This is far from the whole story of music. There have been rich musical cultures among the peoples of Asia and Africa, and the Indian peoples of the Americas. Capitalism, which arose in Europe and the Americas during the past five hundred years, took its riches from the robbery and colonial exploitation of Asia, Africa, and the Americas. This exploitation worked havoc among the native peoples and their cultures. This havoc was accompanied by enslavement of the peoples and contempt for their cultures.

Yet the contribution of the European music of the last five hundred years was a historic and crucial one in the development of the art. This contribution is not to be regarded as the product of any particular culture. It drew heavily upon Asian and African music. The liturgical music of the Middle Ages was based on Catholic chant, which drew upon Greek, Syrian, and Hebrew music. The folk music of eastern, central, and southwestern Europe, which infused the classic musical creations of the last five centuries, was itself built on a heritage of Asian and African music. A basic contribution to the music that has developed in the Americas was made by the Negro people and the culture they brought from Africa. Drawing upon these riches, the great works made possible by the battles of capitalism against feudalism in Europe represent a great and unique advance, which raised the social content of music to a new level, increased the breadth of its forms, and gave it a powerful role in the battle of ideas. There can be no doubt that this classic heritage will be a source of lessons for music in the future, just as there can be no doubt that in the future the people and musical resources of Asia, Africa, and the Americas will play a powerful and independent role.

The organization of sounds in human images was a creation of primitive tribal life.

In primitive social organization the means of livelihood, the hunting and fishing grounds and the land on which crops were raised, were communally possessed; and the wresting of man's needs from nature, the sowing, harvesting, and hunting, were carried on socially by the entire tribe. Nature, still unexplored and unmastered, was seen as peopled by powerful, mysterious, living forces. Along with the first real mastery of nature through the use of fire, the creation of the ax, the spear, the wheel, the boat, and pottery, primitive tribes also attempted to control nature through collective magic rituals. These rituals combined poetry, music, and dance in one set of actions, along with the painting of the body and the carving of masks. What was "magic" about them was the belief that through imitating or symbolizing the mysterious forces of nature by word, gesture, or paint, the tribesmen could assert domination over those forces. With the development of more powerful tools and of real scientific knowledge of the world, magic became utterly fantastic and degenerated into superstition. Yet in primitive life it had a core of realism. It was a means of organizing the tribe's collective labor in real activities such as hunting and sowing, and the beginning of an attempt to understand nature. There were rituals of hunting, war, sowing, harvest, festive initiation of the young into adulthood, and ceremonies over the burial of the dead. Each had its own dance or song.

In tribal rituals appear the two characteristics of organized musical sound, contrasting and yet combining, that are basic to the entire art of music: pitch and rhythm. Pitch refers to the relatively high or low quality of tones, a quality which rises from the fact that the faster the rate of vibration of the sound waves in the air, the higher the tone will sound to the ear. Rhythm refers to the regular recurrence of groups of accents or beats. Although it is possible experimentally to have music on a single repeated tone, all known music uses at least two different tones. Even in speech today a monotone sounds lifeless; it is the presence of pitch, of different intonations, which adds an affecting human feeling to speech. Similarly it is experimentally possible to have a rhythm consisting of a single recurring beat, but practically all known musical rhythm consists of the alternation of at least two different beats, as in the heartbeat, breathing, walking, rowing, the sowing of grain, the up-and-down swing of an ax, and all the movements of labor. It is this alternation, or up-and-back quality of rhythm, which gives it the character not merely of division of time into intervals, but of forward motion.

In primitive rituals, music of pitch and music of rhythm were distinct from one another, although never wholly separate. The words of the rituals were chanted, thus producing a song, although the word "song" had a different meaning from what it has today. A song in primitive life was a melodic phrase seemingly endlessly repeated, with little variation, close to the intonations of speech. It was organized most simply about a single repeated tone as a center or resting place, about which the other tones clustered. Sometimes this tonal center could extend to an axis of two or more repeated tones.

A dance meant a rhythmic pattern also endlessly repeated. The rhythms of primitive music achieved great complexity, inspired by the remarkable skills in manipulating hands, fingers, and feet, and by the complicated cross-motions of the limbs, fingers, head, and body in ritual dance.

There were different songs and dances in primitive life, each having a different use—for hunting, battle, sowing, harvesting, rowing, love-making, or lullaby, for example. Out of the use of such definite musical patterns for human social activities arose the human imagery of music, or the ability of musical patterns to evoke the images of different actions and the feelings associated with them. It is a much debated question whether the human imagery of music is only arbitrary, an outgrowth of social custom, or whether it is based on the natural physical characteristics of sound. It cannot be otherwise than a product of both. Different peoples have different musical patterns for courtship, battle, or putting a child to sleep. These are socially evolved. Yet the fact that sounds are produced by different tensions of the body, of chest, throat, lips, and fingers, indicates that there must be a relation between these body tensions and the affecting quality of the tones they produce. Certainly the music that one people uses for a war cry cannot become a lullaby for others.

It was a great advance, which may have taken place in primitive life, for "songs" to be not merely sung, but played on instruments, such as pipes, and still have the connotations of the words and feelings to which the music was originally set. Music has since gone a long way from song-speech, or the simple reflection of the intonations and accents of speech, and from the bare impact of rhythmic movement. Yet a key to the expressiveness of all music, including the instrumental, is the fact that permanently embedded in it are the speech inflections, patterns of body movement, and human imagery which rose from the fact that it accompanied almost every activity of life. And it is a necessary part of a thriving musical culture that along with the imposing musical forms it produces, music is also used by the people for song, dance, march, the activities of labor, and other aspects of their daily lives. Thus the human imagery of music, the key to its content, is confirmed by people through their very use of it.

Primitive tribal communalism was followed by slaveholding societies. These are sometimes called the first "city civilizations" because of their great temples and palaces, with workshops and homes clustered about them, but the main productive labor was still agricultural. The slave-owners were given titles such as king, emperor, pharaoh, and their military lieutenants and overseers became the landed nobility.

There were constant wars for land and slaves, and also sharp class struggles between slave-owners and slaves, and between the landed nobility and small peasantry. Slave societies include those of ancient Egypt, starting about 3000 B.C., those of Mesopotamia and India, the city-states of ancient Greece, the empire of Alexander, and finally the Roman Empire. These societies produced highly specialized craftsmen, most of whom were slaves, including trained musicians. Elaborate musical instruments were developed, made possible by increasing skills in working metal, wood, and stone, and by increasing mathematical knowledge. The latter made it possible to calculate the pitch of instruments with exactness through the sizes of pipes and strings and the placement of holes. Out of such instrumental development the voice and ear could be trained to hear and reproduce more exact pitch.

Music in these societies was still considered to have magical powers and was used for rituals. The rituals, however, were no longer a collective product of all the people, but were organized by the priesthood in the interests of king and nobility, to affirm the belief that the slaveholders were not ordinary mortals but gods and the descendants of gods.

If on the one hand the music of slave society was more formalized in its rituals, it also provided great advances in instrumental techniques, and an arena for a rich development of the human imagery of music. The traditional musical patterns developed by various tribes could be brought together, thus infusing each other. Epic poems, such as those ascribed to Homer, describing the exploits of tribal kings and chieftains and intermixed with ritual and magic beliefs, were publicly chanted to music. Independent rituals arose among the slaves, peasantry, and mine laborers, such as the Osiris cults of Egypt and the Dionysian and Orphic cults of Greece. The great dramas which flowered out of the Dionysian cults in the Greek city-states, such as Athens, were saturated with music.

The music of slave society, judging from portrayals of groups of musicians, was frequently polyphonic, or many-voiced. Many singers and instrumentalists performed together, and although they might all start with the same traditional melody, each would improvise upon it differently, depending upon the character of his voice or instrument. Thus a music of complicated, interweaving strands could arise, although it was still improvisational, and very different from the highly organized polyphonic music of the Middle Ages. Also in these societies appeared the first attempts at writing music. There is no musical notation in any of these early cultures which sets down pitch and time duration with the exactness demanded by musical composition. Sometimes this early notation was a picturization of the hand and finger motions of the leader of a chorus. Among the Greeks, an elaborate notation was built up based on the position of the fingers in performing on an instrument. Music in these societies was also elaborately rhythmic, reflecting the intricate movements of ritual dances, and using not only a wide variety of drums and taborets but also bells and strings, which produced a music both melodic and percussive. In Africa a rhythmic music developed as a kind of speech communication that could be heard over long distances.

There is music to be heard today which can give us some idea of the character of this ancient music. There is the ritual music of India, with hundreds of melodic and rhythmic patterns, called "ragas" and "talas," each associated with some particular thing such as a god, a "passion" like bravery or tranquility, or a time of the day. There are the Hebrew cantorial chants, with their free vocal arabesques. There is still a rich tradition of poetic-musical improvisation, comprising entire epics, among the Asian peoples. There is the flamenco music of the Spanish folk, with its affecting speechlike intonations, and its intricate guitar rhythms woven about the voice. There is the blues music brought into being by the Negro people of the United States at the end of the nineteenth and beginning of the twentieth century. Such music has ancient roots and is at the same time modern, to the extent that it reflects the feelings and struggles of people today. It is a music partly traditional, in the germ melodic shapes that it uses over and over again, and partly improvisational. It may be analyzed by scholars, but it really does not exist as a body of musical work apart from actual performance, for the performers are themselves creators. Its human imagery is found partly in the traditional melodic germs, which are a social inheritance and creation, and partly in the variations and intense expression of the performer, who is deeply affecting to the hearers for he or she seems to speak the mind of all of them.

2. Village, Court, and Church

MUSIC IN THE MIDDLE AGES, the age of feudalism, took its theory, forms, and practices from slave society and primitive tribal music. Yet these forms were only an outer shell, within which developments of the richest kind took place, which eventually transformed music into an art wholly new in form and content, able to speak to broad audiences and to achieve a full portrayal of life and human character.

As in slaveholding society, the major production of wealth took place on the land. The ruling class of emperor, kings, and landowning lords regarded both the land and their titles of nobility as given to them by divine right, a theory also affirmed and enforced by the medieval church. The free peasantry and serfs, free in the sense that they were not slaves, were almost as tightly bound to the service of their lords, and as restricted in their movements, as the slaves had been, and were subject to poverty, plague, and starvation. Yet there were ways of escape for some of the bold and hardy, who could become outlaws and brigands, or could become the journeymen, artisans, and merchants of the growing towns and cities. The peasants were also able to carry out rebellions on a scale unknown to slave society, and the peasant revolts of the fourteenth, fifteenth, and sixteenth centuries played a powerful role in the dissolution of feudalism. '

The Holy Roman Empire and the papacy were, to lift a phrase from Thomas Hobbes, "the ghost of the deceased Roman Empire, sitting crowned upon the grave thereof." Theoretically, through the hierarchy extending from emperor through kings and lesser nobles down to the serfs, and from pope through cardinal and bishop down to the local priest, the empire and the papacy ruled all Europe. In actual fact, Christendom in the thirteenth and fourteenth centuries was rocked by struggles between emperor and pope over the power that each claimed to wield above the other. Pope, cardinals, and bishops were rich and powerful landowners, nobles, and secular rulers in their own right.

Throughout Europe merchant and manufacturing cities arose which theoretically owed loyalty to church, empire, and the nobility. The population of these cities, the "middle class" of feudalism, were also organized along the lines of a feudal hierarchy, in guilds of the various trades and crafts, with the guild master workmen over the journeymen, and the journeymen over the apprentices. Yet these cities, from behind their stout walls, fought against emperor, pope, and the nobility, both secular and church. They were little republican centers, electing their own mayors, aldermen, burgomasters, and signoria. This relative democracy did not extend, of course, to the poor of the cities, let alone to the peasantry on the land outside. Yet these middle class struggles in the cities were a powerful factor in the breakup of feudalism. They led to the formation of city-states, such as the Republic of Venice and the Commune of Florence. They supported the rise of national states, as in France and England, independent of emperor and pope, and unified against the arrogant claims of the internal nobility.

Music in the Middle Ages still existed in a shell of the "magical." During the fourth century St. Ambrose, Bishop of Milan, engaged in converting people to the church, composed many hymns based on folk strains. He was accused by the purists of "having charmed the people with magic chants."[1] Throughout the Middle Ages the sound of bells was thought to have magic properties, useful for frightening demons. The alchemists used musical symbols as part of their cabalistic mixture of magic and what was later to become chemistry. Yet music in the Middle Ages was also a weapon of struggle. It was divided on class lines, reflecting the classes of feudal society. There were a folk music of the peasantry, a music of the courts, an official music of the church, and a growing music of the city middle class, the bourgeois. Each made an individual and important contribution to musical development.

The richest development of human imagery came from the peasantry. Among the peasantry there existed a heritage of memories passed down by word of mouth, of epic songs and sagas which had been sung by minstrels for the tribal courts at a time when the kings still led their people into battle and did not live very differently from the common people themselves. Many other ceremonies and rituals were carried over from tribal life, such as the carnivals, the spring and harvest dances, maypole dances, courtship and wedding ceremonies. Some of these rituals were absorbed into Christianity, as in the Christmas and Easter celebrations. The "mystery" and "passion" plays, telling of the death and resurrection of Christ, were also a carry-over from tribal ritual, and in fact are very similar to the ancient rituals of Osiris and Dionysius which acted out the death and rebirth of a god. This folk art, however, which combined music and poetry, as well as dance and miming, was no mere half-remembered relic of tribal life. It was needed by the peasantry as an independent culture of their own and a means of struggle against the oppressive forces of feudal life, just as, much later, the Negro slaves in the United States preserved memories of African culture as forms of communication and of struggle against slavery, with meanings known only to the slaves. And so this primitive and tribal art was transformed; it took on as a new content the ways of life, character, and struggles of the medieval peasantry. Ancient sagas became "outlaw" ballads, such as those of Robin Hood, expressing the popular hatred of courts and nobility. Folk religious music-plays and songs, such as the Christmas carols, emphasized not Christ the King, but the common people's symbol of the mother and child in the poor manger, to whom kings did homage. Ballads and songs with cryptic primitive symbols became revolutionary songs of the peasantry, such as the English ballads of the "Cutty Wren," which the people hunted, and of the mystically indestructible "John Barleycorn." There grew up a variety of songs of love, courtship, lullaby, labor in the fields and in village shops. The earthy simplicity and strong human imagery of this music made it of inestimable service to the later development of a powerfully realistic composed music. One of the great contributions of this folk music to the development of the art was that it laid the basis for a national music, a composed music that would sound characteristic and typical of England, France, Italy, Germany, Russia, Bohemia. This growth of folk music and its entrance into "art" music was a continuous process from the fifteenth century to the present day, as struggles for national unification and independence developed in one nation after another.

The culture of the medieval courts was also filled with rituals carried over from more primitive times, although in a manner very different from that of the folk. It is the custom in histories of culture

to describe the court primitivisms and archaisms as things of ineffable
beauty, while those of the folk are characterized as examples of ignorance and superstition, as in the following passage: "It is here that the
path of fancy proved its civilizing value. All aristocratic life in the later
Middle Ages is a wholesale attempt to act the vision of a dream. In
cloaking itself in the fanciful brilliance of the heroism and probity of
a past age, the life of the nobles elevated itself towards the sublime....
The need of high culture found its most direct expression in all that
constitutes ceremonial and etiquette. The actions of princes, even
daily and common actions, all assume a quasi-symbolic form and tend
to raise themselves to the ranks of mysteries. Births, marriages, deaths
are framed in an apparatus of solemn and sublime formalities."[2] If
the rituals of the court, like its costumes, embodied more elaborate
craftsmanship, those of the folk had a more earthy sense of reality.
Just as primitive rituals among the common people gave rise to the
folk play, so among the nobility they gave rise to the court tournaments, a kind of ritual drama of "make-believe of heroism and love."
Just as the ancient sagas gave birth to the outlaw ballads of the folk,
so they also produced the court tales of chivalry in which gallant
knights slew enemies by the thousands with magic swords, killed
dragons and rescued virgins from the castles of magicians. Music and
poetry were part of every courtier's education, like the hunt, dance
and swordplay, and love-making was an elaborate game carried out with
a highly formalized poetry and music.

The great contribution made by the court music of the Middle
Ages was that it combined a vocal, instrumental, and composing skill,
otherwise heard only in church music, with themes that dealt, even if in
partly formalized fashion, with such secular subjects as love, the
beauties of nature, and the exploits of battle. The art of the troubadours
and trouvères of the south of France during the eleventh and twelfth
centuries, poet-musicians and singers connected with the courts, has
been particularly renowned. This Provençal culture leaned toward a
heretical and humanist version of Christian theology. It was wiped
out when the land was devastated in the crusades of 1209 and 1244,
"holy wars" carried on against the prevalent humanist heresies much
feared by the church—the Waldensian and Albigensian. The art was
one in which, as in the sagas and battle songs heard in the tribal courts

of more ancient days, or the Homeric epics of Greece, poetry and music, improvisation and composition, had not yet separated from each other. The music tended to be "endless melody," guided in its form by the stanzas of the poem and by the inflections of speech, adorned with elaborate vocal decorative figures and also making use of folk melody. "The highly skilled art of these wonderful musician-poets was carefully secluded from the uninitiated. They took pride in developing an obscure manner called the *trobar clus* (literally to compose 'closed' or obscurely), yet their sophisticated forms appeal by a spirit of freshness deriving from the simple, rough-hewn examples invented by the people."[3] In the later Middle Ages, although poetry and music remained an avocation of courtiers, court music came increasingly to be composed by skilled artisans hired for the purpose.

The cities, being merchant centers, were focal points in which widely different strains of music could be brought together, to enrich one another. The peasantry brought their folk instruments, and folk songs and dances. There also could be heard the elaborate music composed by church masters for the cathedrals. An independent musical art of the city artisans and middle class grew up, of which little is known because it was frowned upon by the church theorists and scholars of music. "A writer on music about 1300, the Frenchman Johannes de Grocheo, dared, as the first one, to discuss the *musica vulgaris* of Paris, with its songs and dances, along with the dignified music of the Church."[4] Typical of the musical mixtures that could take place were religious chants into the midst of which folk songs found their way, and "motets" in which a traditional religious hymn was sung simultaneously with what were frequently ribald secular songs. In the German cities the mastersingers arose, guild members who prided themselves on their avocation of poetry and music. "The syllabification and tonal character of these pieces, their frank rhythms and simple layout imply a popular and primitive appeal. They anticipate the Lutheran choral which was to appear a century before the reformation."[5] The peasant religious plays with music, both devout and satirically anti-clerical, were taken over and expanded by the city guilds. With the arrival of ships and merchant caravans, music of widely separate lands, of France, England, Germany, Italy, and the East, could intermingle. As the cities, particularly those of Italy, grew in wealth and power, great open-air pageants were presented with music, in which lay some of the beginnings of what was later to become grand opera.

A rich source of song came from the wandering students, who produced a music and poetry full of joy in life, love, and the open road. Even more important in the development of a secular music was the art of the jesters, jongleurs or jugglers, minstrels, actors, and mountebanks who wandered from town to town, welcomed by village, city, and court alike for their entertainment. The word "jester" comes from the old word, *geste-our,* the singer of *gestes* or sagas of the tribal courts. These minstrels were attacked by both church and state authorities; the general charge was that they were immoral, "lascivious," and agents of Satan, but the real motive, as in all such cases of "moral" censorship of a people's art, was political. "By the thirteenth century the minstrel became a powerful factor, loved and feared. In a single person he played the role of newspaper, theatre and music hall."[6] By the fourteenth century, Lang writes, "while the minstrels now enjoyed more freedom than they had in the early Middle Ages, the authorities frowned upon them because they were able, under the guise of singing, to encourage social or political revolt."[7] In 1402 the English House of Commons ordered that "no westours and rimers, minstrels or vagabonds, be maintained in Wales, to make kymorthas or quyllages on the common people, who by their divinations, lies, and exhortations are partly cause of the insurrection and rebellion now in Wales."[8]

It was in the cities, among the guilds of printers, that the practice of printing music arose, enabling musical composition and performance to be spread far and wide and studied in a way previously impossible. The first printed music appeared in 1500 in Venice. It was not, however, until the end of the eighteenth century that composers were able actually to make a living from the printing and sale of their music. A contribution of the cities, which proved to be of the utmost importance in the future transformation of music, was the development of music based on what are our present-day major-minor scales. This system was a simplification of musical writing and thinking, freeing the art of music from the complications and theological rules of the church modes, and at the same time it made possible a new wealth of emotion and drama in music. The major-minor tonalities arose in folk and popular music, and in the cross-pollination of many strains brought by the minstrels and city entertainers. Lang writes: "The oldest docu‧ ments of popular instrumental music testify to the vogue of a major-minor conception of tonality among these simple musicians, a fact which is an exception with the art music of the period. Medieval musical science was contemptuously opposed to these tonalities, against which it cited the doctrines of the ancients."[9]

To the church throughout the Middle Ages music was not an art devoted to the many-sided portrayal of life but part of religious ritual, bound to its words and ceremonies. The Catholic chants themselves, the basis of liturgical music, had arisen between the fourth and ninth centuries out of popular song and ancient Greek, Syrian, and Hebrew chants, but they were standardized by the church theoreticians into various modes, each with its own ritual use, which were presumed to be the modes of ancient Greek music and were given Greek names, such as Dorian, Lydian, and Phrygian. Within church music, however, two great advances took place which were crucial to the development of the art. One was the rise of musical notation, worked out by the monks in the monasteries of the eleventh and twelfth centuries. By the thirteenth century notes were written in exact time values as well as pitch. The basis was laid for the freedom of music from the limitations of improvisation. A musical composition could be studied, worked over, developed in length and breadth, form and content. Improvisation, although it has the excitement of being stimulated directly by the impact of an audience, necessarily advances slowly, repeating traditional patterns over and over again, adding only slight nuances to them. And along with musical notation rose the composer, the creator of finished and permanent musical works. For some centuries composers still wrote only "parts" for the various singers, as if the music were still partly to be improvised. But by the fifteenth century composers began to write in "score," putting down all the different vocal parts on the same page, thus enabling them to conceive the work better in terms of its simultaneous sounds as well as its melodic lines.

The church of the Middle Ages was itself the greatest of landowners and the staunch support of feudalism. It fostered the composer of music for its own glory and for the grip that music could have on people's minds. It trained gifted children of the poor to become singers, composers, in its ranks. Musical craft and theory in the Middle Ages were a branch of theology, like painting, education, philosophy, law, and what passed for science. There was no other place to which the composer could go. The liturgical mass and motet became the major musical forms of the age, constantly growing in architectural breadth. Yet in fostering musical composition, the church brought a force into being that would eventually break the ecclesiastical grip upon music itself. As one creative musical mind after another appeared, each building on his predecessor's work, each seeking to make music meaningful in its human imagery and emotional content, the demands of ritual increasingly appeared to be manacles that had to be broken. The composers came from different social classes. Guillaume de Machault (1300-1370?) was a French courtier and diplomat. Guillaume Dufay (1400-1474), another great French composer, was born of peasant folk, and his music has a folkish loveliness and simplicity of melody that makes it the most lovable of the Middle Ages. To the church, all music was theoretically supposed to sound the same, built on the same modes and rituals, no matter in what land it appeared. Yet a national character forced its way into composed music, mainly into that for secular use but not ignoring the liturgical. Almost all of the great church composers wrote secular music. Machault wrote songs and ballads, and Dufay also wrote many enchanting songs and dances. The great composer of the Netherlands, Orlando di Lasso (1532-1594), wrote hundreds of chansons, madrigals, and comic and satiric villanelles, or dancing songs. The Flemish composer Isaak (1450?-1517) wrote carnival songs to be sung in the streets of Florence. Yet the secular music, if it was able to catch the varied human imagery, and the sunny and serious moods of daily life, was still bound to the short and restricted forms of dance music and settings for lyric poetry. Had poets been restricted in the same way to sonnets and songs, the results would have been beautiful, but the full exploration of life, the battle of ideas, the striving to move great audiences with great experiences, would have been impossible. This required forms of greater breadth, such as Dante created in his *Divine Comedy* and Shakespeare in his dramas. Composed music under feudalism was divided into two parts, each inadequate; in that of the church could be found the greatest grandeur of form and applied knowledge of composition, but dedicated

to the "after life"; in that of secular song and dance could be found
something of the many-sided experiences of life, but limited to vig-
nettes and miniatures, and addressed largely to the service of the
courts and the upper middle class.

This is not to say that the church music of feudalism was devoid of
human imagery. The church may have fostered composition and
musical theory in order to attack folk music and eliminate improvisation, with its dreaded intrusion of national, "pagan," and secular
images. Throughout the Middle Ages folk music was called an arm
of Satan, and Satan himself was pictured as enticing people to perdi-
tion with a fiddle in his hands. Something of this was recognized by
Samuel Wesley, the English hymn composer, centuries later, when he
said he didn't see "why the devil should have the best tunes." But the
"devil" entered church music itself. The music would have had little
quality, other than a pale, ethereal decoration of the words, had not
its composers felt that religion to them involved people's life and needs
in the real world as well as the next one. The monks in the monasteries
put love songs between the drawn-out syllables of liturgical chants. The
folk improvised "motets" combining church chants with ribald songs.
Dufay put lovely French folk songs into his church masses. Between
the thirteenth and sixteenth centuries a perpetual battle was waged
between church authorities and musicians over the injection of folk
songs and dances and folk-style music into liturgical composition. This
pressure for folk and secular elements in church music was not merely
a humanization of ritual. It had connotations of politics and class
struggle. The "battle for the Bible," to translate the Bible into vernacular languages and to interpret religion in terms of the needs of the
common people, was one of the forms taken by the struggle of the
peasantry, the weavers and masons, the city middle classes, against
the courts, nobility, wealthy merchants, and the church itself. Engels
writes: "The Middle Ages had attached to theology all the other forms
of ideology—philosophy, politics, jurisprudence—and made them sub-
divisions of theology. It therefore constrained every social and political
movement to take on a theological form. To the masses whose minds
were fed with religion to the exclusion of all else, it was necessary to
put forward their own interests in a religious guise in order to produce
a great agitation."[10]

There was no question in the Middle Ages as to whether music had real and specific meanings. In 1325, a bull of Pope John XXII denounced the "new school" of music which "invented new melodies in a new notation rather than singing old ones, forced rapid tempos on sacred music, dissolved the melody by ornaments, rests and polyphony, and grafted sacred words on secular tunes; in short, it disturbed devotion, intoxicated the ear, and perverted the listener."[11] These were exactly the ways in which folk melody had entered sacred music, by becoming vocal "ornaments" to traditional chants and becoming polyphonic vocal lines sung simultaneously with them. In the sixteenth century a secret musical language grew up in the church music of the Netherlands composers, with hints to singers that certain passages were to be performed in altered fashion from the way in which they were written, and with other musical devices used to emphasize certain words in the text, "hiding views that the church was not supposed to discover."[12] With the ordinances of the Council of Trent (1545-63), called to combat the rising tide of Protestantism, Catholic liturgical music was "purified." The effect of this purification, however, was only to drive the best composers into writing more and more for secular purposes.

Protestant music was a development of these folk, national, and heretical elements in the music of the Catholic Church. Martin Luther created a body of hymns in part adapted from folk songs, in part composed in popular style by himself and other German composers. These hymns or "chorales" took on the character of a national music of the German middle class. They were also battle songs of the peasantry in the historic revolt of 1525. A large part of the middle class joined the nobles and turned viciously against the peasantry. During the two centuries of war and economic stagnation that followed, which served to strengthen the power of the German princes, these chorales remained in German popular and sacred music as a relic and reminder of the time when the German people had almost broken the bonds of feudalism.

During the sixteenth and early seventeenth century leading composers appeared, such as Orazio Vecchi (1550?-1605) in Italy, John Dowland (1562-1626), Thomas Morley (1557-1603), and John Wilbye (1574-1638) in England, who devoted all or almost all of their talents to secular music. The music they wrote—madrigals, instrumental dances, and "chamber music" to be performed in the homes—was still in part the endless melody of older times, guided in its movement by the inflections of poetry, but with a fine interweaving of many vocal and instrumental strands. At the same time, within this art a new form of the solo song developed, a song that was no longer a phrase endlessly repeated or an improvisation on a set pattern, but a tonally organized work with a beginning, middle, and end apparent to the ear. As composers paid increasing attention to the merged sounds produced by many voices, and to the movement from one tonal center to another, the major-minor scales began to suffuse all music, even that of leading Catholic liturgical composers such as Palestrina (1526-1594) in Italy, although the theorists tried to show by all sorts of ingenious manipulations of the old official church modes that the music was still being written within these modes.

The evolution of self-contained, rounded melody, out of the looser forms of improvised ritual, song-speech and "endless melody," made possible a more objective musical form. The melody was recognized by the listeners as not merely a series of notes, but as a unit of human imagery, speaking of a joy, sorrow, love and lamentation that they could relate to their own lives. As such, it could both serve in their daily lives, as songs to sing, and be used by composers as a building element in larger musical structures.

The close of the Middle Ages and the battles of capitalism against feudalism were marked out in culture by the breaking of the grip of theology over all forms of thought, including the arts. Art could deal with religious themes, but its main task now had to be the study of life in terms of life itself, and its central subject had to be the human being, studied from real life.

The Renaissance secularization of art showed itself in one historic musical development, the appearance of music drama, or grand opera, at the end of the sixteenth century. This was the first form in the history of music which could take on the many-sided investigation of secular life and human character, with a breadth of form and architecture equal to and surpassing that of church music.

3. The Composer as Artist and Artisan

TO EXTRACT THE MEANING of the music of the seventeenth and eighteenth centuries becomes a problem of penetrating the outer form in which it superficially clothes itself. From the point of view of a later age, everything seems to have been topsy-turvy. Musical works of the deepest thought and most searching emotion are offered simply as "exercises" for the instruction of the young, as technical treatises, or as "chamber music" for the diversion of amateurs at home. Classical or "serious" opera, pretending to be lofty tragedy cut to fit the tastes of the proudest nobility, is actually most infantile in story and characterization. Comic opera, offering itself as light entertainment, contains the most serious social thinking and the most realistic human images. Great musicians in the truest sense of the word "great," profound thinkers in musical form and content, are treated by the feudal aristocracy, for whom they work, as artisans and servants in livery, hardly above the status of a cook. Religious music, which in a previous age had fought against the intrusion of folk and secular elements, now embraces every kind of song and dance music, borrowing heavily from opera, in order to hold its audiences. Great dramatic and intricate musical structures, embodying encyclopedic studies in harmony and musical form, are offered superficially as collections of dances, for, to the feudal aristocracy who control most musical production, all music must apparently sound like a light and jigging dance.

In this apparent contradiction between content and form, the music reflects the conditions of real life of the age. The economic life of England, France, Italy, and Germany is mercantile and capitalist. Yet everywhere but in England, the state forms are hangovers of feudalism, dominated by monarchies with elaborate and wasteful courts, and by

24

an equally wasteful and parasitical landed aristocracy living on the backs of the peasantry. Even in England, where the revolution of 1648 accelerated the development of capitalism, the state is run by a combination of great landowners and wealthy merchants.

Typical of the contradictions affecting the music of the age are those seen in opera. Opera, or drama set to music, appeared in Florence and Venice at the turn of the sixteenth century, seemingly wrapped in the authority of antiquity, as a "revival" of classic Greek drama, the poetry of which was known to have been chanted. It proved to be a most popular commercial musical entertainment, and within a few years there were seventeen opera houses in Venice alone. It became the favored entertainment at all the courts of Europe, existing at the mercy of court politics, becoming a form through which kings and nobility could patronize music, dictate its form and content, and yet have it partially supported by the public. The Italian cities, declining as merchant empires, became training grounds for singers, instrumental performers, composers, and libretto writers, who were exported almost like luxuries such as laces and wines. Opera became a cosmopolitan art of the dream world of feudalism, almost the same in story, and often in music and language, in whatever land it was presented. The world it presented was one of a fancied past, in which time stood still, merchants, capitalists, workers, and rebellious peasantry were non-existent, and only noble characters, garbed as ancient heroes or demi-gods, such as Achilles, Orpheus, Hector, and Roland, told of their exploits, passions, and heartbreaks. The music in which they thus declaimed and lamented generally sounded strangely like refined or sentimentalized folk songs and dances. The characterizations, in poetry and music, had necessarily to become one-sided and shallow, abstractions of love, sorrow, or anger. The high point of an operatic presentation frequently became the elaborate stage spectacle itself, with trap-doors opening in the stage floor, live waterfalls playing, angels or goddesses strapped to wires flying through the air, and exotic ballets.

An illustration of the slow development of the form under these circumstances was the fact that one of the very earliest composers of opera and a groundbreaker in the medium, Claudio Monteverdi (1567-1643), who began his career as a viola player to the Duke of Mantua, remained unsurpassed in the musical portrayal of emotion and character in "serious" opera for the next two centuries. He drew upon a rich variety of musical resources to make his human beings live on the stage, including a free-flowing song-speech or "recitative" reminiscent of old court ballads and church music, the art of the madrigals, songs for solo voice, dances, and songs in folk style, and developed the harmonic and instrumental colors of the orchestra accompanying the voices. In most of the operas after him the music becomes a declamation of poetry alternating with a kind of concert in costume of dances and songs, or "airs," with elaborate improvisational passages, or "cadenzas," in which the singers could display their technical agility. The "arias" or airs for solo voice were frequently in the rhythm of such dances as gavottes, minuets, or sicilianas. This was engaging enough to the ear, but it somewhat limited their power to portray emotional conflict and to plumb the depths of feeling. In the latter eighteenth century the composer Christoph Willibald von Gluck (1714-1787) issued a manifesto declaring that in opera "the true mission of music was to second the poetry, by strengthening the expression of the sentiments and increasing the interest of the situations." The real trouble, however, lay not in the fitness of the music to the words but in the words themselves, protected from all realism and sense by the censorship of the aristocracy which controlled the theater. The operas of men of genius such as Jean Phillippe Rameau (1683-1764) in France, George Frederick Handel (1685-1759) in England, and Gluck, who wrote in Milan, Venice, Vienna, and Paris, for all the inspired music in them, are unplayable today, because of the feudal ritual to which they were bound in music, word, and action. What the aristocracy of the time felt to be the last word in drama seems now to be silly and infantile.

In spite of the shallow conception of human beings and human relations that prevailed in the opera known as classical or "serious," because of its stately ritual and simulation of poetic tragedy, the form made an important contribution to the development of music. It encouraged the development of skilled singers and instrumentalists. It inspired the formation of large bodies of fine instrumentalists, which finally broke away from the opera house to become the magnificent collective instrument, the symphony orchestra, of later times. Even the comparatively shallow reflection of human passions in instrumental form, which rose in opera, inspired the development of the orchestral symphony, which may be called a dramatic work for orchestra without words. The word "symphony" comes from "sinfonia," which was an orchestral overture or introduction to a dramatic vocal work. The rise of skilled instrumentalists, and the interplay of solo singers with the accompanying orchestra, inspired the development of the instrumental concerto, a work in which the proclamation of musical themes by the full orchestra alternated with improvisations and developments of these themes by one or a group of solo instrumentalists, displaying their skill in technique and musical invention. One of the greatest of early concerto composers, Antonio Vivaldi (1675?-1743) who wrote in Venice, dramatically entitled one of his series of twelve concertos "The Contest between Harmony and Invention," describing the form as a test of skill, alternating the "harmonies" announced by the full orchestra with the "inventions" upon these harmonies by the solo passages. The concertos also sparkled with many passages of nature imagery, inspired by opera, music simulating winds, the play of water, storms, dances of spring, and hunting horns. This movement of dramatic ideas into instrumental music was one of the ways in which composers slowly began to create a kind of music reflecting the bourgeois world view and human image. They began to see the world as a place of conflict, instead of seeking a dream escape to a fancied peace and "simplicity," as the aristocracy was doing.

If the invention of opera may be called a revolt against the domination of music by the church, so the phenomenal development of instrumental music of the late seventeenth and early eighteenth centuries may be called a revolt against the aristocratic censorship of opera. The forms of this instrumental music often rise directly out of opera or other vocal music, and at the same time become more truly dramatic than most opera. Thus out of the sweeping, showy, and "soul-searching" aria of Italian opera rose the instrumental concerto, to which Italian composers made so great a contribution. The overture to Italian opera became an early model for the orchestral symphony. The ballets, or sets of dances, of French opera inspired the instrumental suite, consisting of an overture and a set of dance movements, which in turn helped preside over the birth of the symphony. Divertimentos, or "street serenade" music, arose as an instrumental setting of popular song and dance music. The sonata, which originally meant music to be sounded on an instrument rather than sung, became a major form of musical experiment, generally designed for intimate musical gatherings. Just as opera had stimulated a phenomenal development of the human voice as a performer of music, so these instrumental forms stimulated an equally remarkable development of instrumental technique, and of instruments themselves. The great musicians, middle class composer-servants of the aristocracy, generally showed two faces to their era. They were entertaining "performers," "improvisers," craftsmen to their patrons, but to their fellow composers they were artists, profound inventors, admired thinkers in music.

Comic opera mushroomed in the seventeenth and the eighteenth centuries as a kind of opposite and complement to "serious" or tragic opera. It drew upon the popular folk play and improvised vaudeville, such as the Italian *commedia dell'arte,* the English ballad opera, and the German *singspiel,* with spoken dialogue instead of poetic declamation. It grew to be a double-edged artistic weapon. It enabled the aristocracy to laugh at the buffoonery of the "simple folk." Yet much of the actual shape, color, manners of life, and national consciousness of the times entered into these comic works, and the "simple folk," through ad-libbing and veiled satire, were able to send pointed shafts back at their patrons. In England John Gay's (1685-1732) ballad opera, *The Beggar's Opera,* practically swept grand opera off the stage, although the latter was supplied by so great a musical genius as Handel. Oratorio was created by an Italian Jesuit, St. Philip Neri, as an attempt to combine the popular operatic style with Biblical subjects for Catholic propaganda. Yet the greatest series of oratorios were the Protestant works written by Handel in England to Old Testament subjects, such as *Israel in Egypt, Samson, Saul,* and *Judas Maccabaeus,* celebrating the military victories of the middle class Whigs over their feudal enemies at home and on the European continent. The "cantata," which originally meant simply a piece of music to be sung, developed in Germany as a grand and spacious work of dramatic music, without costumes or scenery, based on a Biblical text, and embodying in its music the great national music of the Lutheran chorales, along with elements taken from opera and from the earthly vitality of folk song. It is typical of the contradictions of the age that these works, such as the cantatas of Bach and the oratorios of Handel, although not designed for the theater, have a more genuinely dramatic music, with deeper tragic feelings and captivating joy in life, than most of the operas of their time. The human imagery of this music is found in its melody and in its great dramatic portrayals of emotion, reflecting the personality and feelings of the bourgeois minds who created it. For Handel in England to turn from opera in Italian to oratorio in English, taking his themes from the Protestant Bible which had been an ideological weapon of the middle class revolution, was a giant advance in both content and form. It was hailed as such by the English population, which accepted these works as a cultural expression of the rise and strength of their own nation. This reflection of bourgeois-democratic thought gives depth to the music of Bach, Handel, and Mozart. The superficial outer imagery is still imposed by feudal myth and ritual—in opera the aristocratic myth of a "chivalry" that had never existed, in oratorio and cantata a religious symbolism and ritual, in comedy the mask of the jester and buffoon behind which shafts of political and social satire were sharpened.

In musical form and technique, the revolutionary achievement of this era was the development and standardization of the system of major and minor scales, "key" and "key change." This was one of the turning points in the history of music, one of the few true advances in the art, which did not merely sharpen a tool, but transformed the art as a medium for the reflection of life.

The important change was the concept of key and of shifting tonality. Under the new system, any chosen tone could serve as the basis of a major or minor scale, and as the tonal center on which a work of music began and ended. This tonic note, or tonal center, became the "key" of the music. The music, in its course, could constantly "modulate" or shift its tonal center, and build powerful emotional and dramatic effects in the contrast between one tonality and another. With the development of "equal temperament," or the tuning of instruments so that there were twelve exactly even half-steps between a note and its octave, it was possible in one composition to move through a cycle of different and connected keys. Thus musical tones could be organized into a kind of solar system, with every possible combination related to every other by innumerable harmonic pulls and tensions. It was possible to organize music harmonically in a way impossible before, using the term "harmony" to refer not only to the merged sounds or "chords" at each particular moment, but the entire pattern of shifting tonalities, the movement away from the first tonal center and the return "home." If the movement from tone to tone in primitive song-speech represented a kind of affective sharpening of each word like a speech intonation, now the movement from key to key, moving and shifting entire blocks of sound, could represent a far richer interplay of mood and emotion, a portrayal of the human mind itself in its awareness of deep conflicts in the world outside and its search for their resolution.

This system may be compared to the development of light and shade, perspective, atmosphere, depth, and the portrayal of human psychology in painting. It made possible a new level of "realism" in music, which in the rising bourgeois world meant an art centered on the study of the human being and human mind, taken from life, and guided in its form by nothing other than the movement, conflicts, storms, and even unanswered questions that arose in the struggles of capitalism against feudalism.

Once established, such a system, like the realistic developments in painting, could be petrified by innumerable useless academic rules, which is indeed what happened to it in the music schools of the nineteenth and twentieth centuries. It could be used not only to explore reality but to simulate emotions and dramas which the composer did not really feel. Every advance in realism, in all of the arts, has given birth to countless fakeries and misuse of the new powers and techniques it gave the artist. Then, as has happened today, reactionary trends arise which point to this and demand that realism itself be thrown out and the art "go back" to the feudal or primitive. An academy of petrified realistic tools is replaced by an academy of even more petrified archaic tools, which seem to be novel only because they have become strange.

The major-minor system was necessary for the further maturity of music as an art. It was developed in the search of the most groundbreaking minds for musical tools that could be used for the reflection of real life. It was not a musical "cosmopolitanism," imposing the same practices, forms, and content upon musicians of all countries. It arose, on the contrary, in combat against the cosmopolitan feudal musical ritual, such as that imposed by the medieval theologians. It helped develop 'national qualities in music, accompanying the rise of nations themselves, as may be seen in the work of Monteverdi, Girolamo Frescobaldi (1583-1644), and Antonio Vivaldi (1675?-1743) in Italy, Henry Purcell (1658-1695) and Handel in England, Diedrich Buxtehude (1637-1707) and Johann Sebastian Bach (1685-1750) in Germany, Jean-Baptiste Lully (1632-1687) and Rameau in France. These composers learned from one another, and even adopted new countries, as Lully moved from Italy to France, Handel from Germany to England, Buxtehude from Sweden to Germany. Yet they drew upon the riches of folk music in the country in which they lived, and created new works that were absorbed by the people as a folk and popular national music.

A great many of the songs for solo voice and operatic airs that appeared in the seventeenth century have a major-minor sound to the ear. In fact, it is this harmonic quality that causes them to sound like a song to the modern ear, as against the song-speech and endlessly weaving melodic line that characterized most of the song of the Middle Ages. At the end of the seventeenth and beginning of the eighteenth century the major-minor system was fully explored in theory and practice by a group of composer-theoreticians who offered their work, actually an exploration of new realms of emotional portrayal in music, as a "science" of music. These men, such as François Couperin (1668-1733), Vivaldi, Buxtehude, Rameau, and Bach, were middle class musical artisans who worked necessarily for the church and aristocracy, but pushed the boundaries of music far beyond the desires of their patrons. They were complete masters of their craft who were virtuosos on the organ and almost every other musical instrument of their time. They frequently trained and led choirs, taught music, improvised and composed, sought out each other's works for study. One medium they used for their harmonic explorations was the "figured bass" or "continuo," a bass melodic line dominating the entire composition, above which an intricate structure of melody and rhythm could be erected, guided in its movement by the harmonic tensions created as it moved away from and back to the tonality of the bass. These leading composers, treated by their patrons as hired servants, were among the great intellects of their time. Almost all of them created works of theory, either in the form of written texts or of sets of musical works designed to explore the resources of the art. They laid the basis for the immense growth of instrumental music by developing such forms as the concerto, sonata, chorale-prelude, toccata, fugue, and dance suite. Many of the more deeply emotional works of the time for organ or bodies of strings were called "fantasias" as if, in the musical world still paying lip service to feudalism, the reflection of something approaching the agitation and conflicts of real life had to be explained as a "fantasy" or a dream. In their concerto recitals, or organ recitals like those Buxtehude and Bach gave in the churches open to the public, or oratorio performances like Handel's in the public theaters, they fostered the development of the middle class concert hall.

The greatest of these composer-theoreticians was Johann Sebastian Bach, and in his life and work the two rival concepts of the musician, the bourgeois artist addressing multitudes and the feudal craftsman-servant, are in conflict, one struggling to break through the shell of the other. He worked for part of his life in the service of the German courts, like those of the Duke of Weimar and the Prince of Anhalt-Köthen, and part as a teacher of music, organist, and composer of Lutheran church services for the city of Leipzig. Living under vestiges of medieval serfdom, he had to get permission every time he changed his job, or even traveled from one town to another. The burghers of the town council of Leipzig, while seeking pious sentiments rather than light entertainment in music, were hardly less conservative and stuffy than the courts. Typical of the conditions under which Bach worked are the terms of the certificate of his appointment as town organist under the Duke of Weimar. "Now therefore you are, above all, to be true, faithful, and obedient to him, His above-mentioned Noble Grace, the Count, and especially to show yourself industrious and reliable in the office, vocation, and practice of art and science that are assigned to you, not to mix in other affairs and functions."[1]

It is not true to say that he was unrecognized by his time, and wrote only for "posterity." This myth, that great artists are never appreciated in their lifetime and work only for the "future," is one of the romantic inventions of the nineteenth century, designed to obscure the fact that composers, although their work is perfectly comprehensible, starve because music is not a profitable business commodity. Very few of

Bach's works were printed in his lifetime. Printing of music was still haphazard, and works of music were not yet accepted as "art," with lasting interest. Yet those that were published in his lifetime caused a great stir, and there was hardly anyone with anything to do with music in Germany, and to some extent all Europe, who did not know him as one of the great musicians of the time.

If Bach was an artisan-servant to some, he was a philosopher, reflecting life in music, to others. A criticism and rebuttal which were written in his lifetime reveal these two conflicting worlds of music most clearly. A critic, Scheibe, attacked Bach in 1737 as a *musikant* and *künstler,* or artisan of music, whose works were too complicated and difficult to perform, and who even went so far as to write down all the notes to be played, instead of leaving room for others to improvise. Scheibe was hotly answered by another musician, Birnbaum, who objected that a word like *musikant* or *künstler* "sounds too much like a handicraftsman, and that to speak thus is just as contrary to the usage of language once introduced as it would be to call philosophers, orators and poets *künstler* in thinking, speaking and verse making.... For this composer does not lavish his splendid ornaments on drinking songs, lullabies, or other insipid *galanteries. . . .* The essential aims of true art are to imitate Nature, and, where necessary, to aid it."[2] He went on to explain that music had other purposes than light entertainment or amateur use, and the expression of profound thoughts in music required exact notation and accomplished performance.

The argument is not really between two differing critiques of a great man, but between two worlds of music, one dying, already an anachronism, and the other struggling to be born. It is true that today, when vistas of a new kind of cultural life are opening up, there need be no opposition between composing for amateur use and also composition on the highest levels of profound content and form. It is ironic however that today, in the name of "Back to Bach," musicians and theoreticians are arguing for a return exactly to the feudalisms of musical "handicraft" against which Bach and the most progressive musicians of his time rebelled.

These contradictions may be found in Bach's music itself. The complicated textures, the knotty problems of construction which Bach solved and for which he is famous, are less signs of a "new form"

arising out of a "new content," than of an attempt to express a new
content by stretching to the utmost the archaic forms imposed upon
him by the conditions under which he had to work. Thus many of
Bach's techniques proved to be unusable to the generation of composers who followed him, and all attempts to revive these forms
today, in the name of "Back to Bach" or "neo-classicism," only result
in the most stuffy, dry, or superficial music. Therein lies the difficulty
of extracting the "meaning" of his music, for the very forms imposed
by feudal culture in its decline are a sort of censorship, and what are
really problems of content and human imagery, the portrayal in
music of a new human imagery and new emotional stirrings, show
themselves superficially as adaptations of set methods of work which
feudal practice regarded as fixed and not to be questioned. The new
pretends that it is really carrying out the old ways with slight
differences.

Thus most of Bach's instrumental works were offered simply as
works for training performers, musical diversion, "keyboard practice,"
and instruction, such as the *Little Organ Book,* the Partitas, the Inventions, the *Well-Tempered Clavier* and the *Art of the Fugue.* The last
named was printed without any instrumentation, as if it were a
treatise on composition meant only for fellow composers to read with
the eye. The *Well-Tempered Clavier* consisted of two sets of twenty-
four preludes and fugues, proceeding in regular order "through all the
tones and semitones," both in major and minor. It was designed to
prove the advantages of the equal-tempered keyboard. What it really
did was to explore the structural and expressive possibilities opened up
by the major-minor system; the movement from key to key in each
single work, the harmonic interplay of a freely moving melodic line
against a solid bass, the expressive use of half-step or "chromatic"
deviations from the major-minor scales. Almost every variety of
musical writing and imagery of the time is contained within them;
showy and glittering finger-display pieces, court and peasant dances,
somber works in the manner of the Lutheran chorales, deeply introspective and poignant pieces that may almost be called musical self-
portraits. And all this was offered simply "For the use and profit of
the musical youth desirous of learning." Bach may be called the
greatest of musical teachers, who, kin to the Encyclopedists of the

eighteenth century, arranged and put into systematic and usable order all the isolated and progressive musical advances of the previous century. Needless to say, he saw these advances not merely as techniques but as means for bringing a richer reflection of human life and drama into music. Only under those conditions could greatness of musical composition take the apparent form of works of instruction.

A great number of his compositions were in dance forms, although the structural complications and emotional depth go far beyond the boundaries of dance. This practice, found also in many of the opera and oratorio arias of Handel and Purcell, was a bow to feudal practice, as if all music had to pretend to be court entertainment, or to proceed in jigging rhythms. The portrayal of human drama and emotional conflict in music required contrasts and oppositions of patterns of movement, and many of Bach's fugues were masterpieces in the interplay of inner rhythms, while the fixed rhythm which dominates the whole becomes almost a ghostly shell. His collections of dance pieces, such as the English Suites, French Suites, Suites for Orchestra, and Goldberg Variations (written to soothe a patron's insomnia) have an encyclopedic quality, collecting and analyzing almost every variety of dance form found in European music.

The fugue form itself, which Bach used so prolifically, was in part archaic. The fugue may be described briefly as a form laid out for a number of separate, interweaving "voices," each entering in turn with the same theme or "subject," and each preserving its identity throughout the work, as if it were still medieval polyphony with each singer having an independent part. Although the separate lines are still called "voices," the fugue may be written for instruments or a single instrument. The "counterpoint," or interweaving of lines, was highly organized on harmonic principles, or the movement away from and back to the starting tonality. Thus the fugue was needed by Bach as a form in which the investigation of new emotional expressions and structural ideas could proceed seemingly in an ancient, accepted garb.

The forms of Protestant church service, such as the cantatas and passions, were archaic even in Bach's time, for there was hardly a flicker left in his Germany of the social upheaval of the Reformation which had given birth to them. The passions even had hangovers of the medieval anti-Semitism which the church and nobility had injected into the story of Christ, in order to channelize the bitter resentments of the peasantry away from themselves and into pogroms against the Jews. Yet they have some of Bach's very greatest music, the rather uninspired, flat poetry contrasting strikingly to the musical imagery, bursting with life and full of dramatic expressions of earthly love, joy, anguish, alarm, tragic despair, pastoral serenity, and folkish high spirits.

Something of the meaning of these works can be gathered from Frederick Engels' description of the desolate state of Germany during Bach's century. "Peasantry, tradesmen, and manufacturers felt the double pressure of a blood-sucking government and bad trade; the nobility and the princes found that their incomes, in spite of the squeezing of their inferiors, could not be made to keep pace with their increasing expenditure. . . . No education, no means of operating upon the minds of the masses, no free press, no public spirit, not even an extended commerce with other countries—nothing but mean-ness and selfishness—a mean, sneaking, miserable shop-keeping spirit pervading the whole people. Everything worn out, crumbling down, going fast to ruin, and not even the slightest hope of a beneficial change, not even so much strength in the nation as might have suf-ficed for carrying away the putrid corpses of dead institutions."[3] It was common talk in Bach's time that a German musician, to make his way, had to go to another country. His son, Karl Philip Emanuel, said of his father, "But in general he did not have the most brilliant good fortune, because he did not do what it requires, namely roam the world over."[4]

Bach's church music had a deep national consciousness. At its heart were the great Lutheran chorales that had been the battle cries of the Reformation. These Bach expands with all that is most dramatic, ex-pressive, human in imagery, and forward-looking in his musical art— impassioned love music, poignant outcries, sunny folk songs and dances. Thus in these works, as in all of his great music, Bach reflects the desolate Germany of his time by speaking over its head, at once looking backward to the heroic days when great German struggles were taking place against feudalism, and looking forward, within this archaic shell exploring the realistic portrayal of human beings and emotional conflicts in music that would be used by composers for the next two hundred years. The harmonic elements in his music are those that would be exploited by the bourgeois revolutionist Beethoven, as well as carried to an extreme of subjectivism by Brahms and Wagner. Bach was a great bourgeois mind, in a time and age when no bourgeois struggles were taking place, when a moribund feudalism still dominated musical culture, and he had to appear to be its "honest servant."

Many of the leading musical intellects of the eighteenth century were born among the petty-bourgeoisie or peasantry. Thomas Britton, an English coal peddler, was one of the founders of public concerts, fixing up his loft as a music room where the public could hear such great musicians as Handel, at a price of one penny. The son of a shoemaker, Johann Nikolaus Forkel, wrote one of the first great critical studies of music, a biography, critique, and appreciation of Bach. Emanuel Schikaneder, a self-educated strolling actor, became one of the most enterprising theatrical producers in Austria, offering Schiller and Shakespeare to the common public, sponsoring and producing one of Mozart's greatest operas, *The Magic Flute,* and stimulating Beethoven to write opera. The giant of the later eighteenth century who did most to cast off the shell of archaic and obsolete musical practices was the son of a peasant wheelright and largely self-educated, Franz Joseph Haydn (1732-1809). Writing mainly for orchestra, for piano, and for string quartet of two violins, viola, and cello, he developed a musical form based on harmonic movement, dynamic and rhythmic contrasts, which began to follow no other rule or pattern than the movement and emotional drama of real people in a real world.

This—the development of the orchestral symphony, the string quartet, and the general principle of formal organization known as "sonata form"—was the next stage in the development of the major-minor harmonic system as a means for reflecting the real world of human struggle. The figured bass or bass continuo of the earlier generation of composers was discarded as no longer necessary, along with a mass of intricate counterpoint, pseudo-scientific theorizing, and the enslavement of so much musical form to dance rhythm. Folk song and folk dance remained, of course, and were even more richly used as a human imagery. Melody became dominant in musical form, supported by shifting harmonies which could add a variety of emotional "colors" to it, and the structure of an entire work was built on powerful dramatic contrasts of melody, massed instrumental sound, rhythms and harmonic movement. These new concepts of musical form were not the product of one man alone. Important figures in the rise of this music were Bach's sons, Johann Christian (1735-1782) and Karl Philip Emanuel (1714-1788), and the Bohemian-born composer, Johann Stamitz (1707-1757). Haydn however, along with the younger genius who learned from him, Mozart, saw the rich possibilities of this development, which seemed to others to be only a "simplification" of music.

A unique quality of Haydn's art was his tie to the peasantry, bringing to his composed music a wealth of middle European, Austrian, and Slovak folk music. He saw this folk material not as comedy, or as a pastoral excursion among the "simple folk," but as material for the most exalted and dramatic musical composition. Haydn also had to work as a servant of the nobility. For a time he almost starved. He was fortunate in finding as a patron one of the wealthiest of European noblemen, Prince Nicholas Esterhazy, who had a private theater and orchestra of skilled musicians, and was willing to allow Haydn to experiment. In spite of Esterhazy's genuine admiration for Haydn's music, the composer had to suffer the many petty tyrannies of a feudal prince who regarded even the greatest of living musicians as a private servant. But the prince had better taste than the critics in Vienna. These critics, who served as censors and cultural spies for the ruling class, seized upon what was precisely one of Haydn's greatest achievements for their condemnation—his use of folk themes in composition in the grand manner. They accused him of "mixing the comic with the serious." Folk art to them was synonymous with "comic." During Haydn's lifetime music began to be published with fair regularity, and it was his growing fame in England and France which finally forced the arbiters of Austrian cultural life to accept him as a great man.

Wolfgang Amadeus Mozart (1756-1791) was the opposite and complement to Haydn. Whereas Haydn was born among the peasantry, Mozart was born in aristocratic and court circles, not himself a prince, of course, but the son of a proficient court musician, who took him throughout Europe as an infant musical prodigy and planned a career for his son in his own footsteps. Before he was ten, Mozart had as much craft as had taken Haydn thirty hard years to learn. He had less of Haydn's warm folk sympathies, being even in childhood a sophisti-

cate and a master of the courtly "galant" style. He became one of the
fine critical intellects of the eighteenth century, like a musical Voltaire,
with the utmost contempt for a feudal order that had become completely corrupt and irrational, and he turned the feudal mannerisms
into satire against feudalism itself. He and Haydn loved, respected,
and learned from each other's work. Both of them joined the Masons,
which was a secret and persecuted anti-feudal order, although some
liberal aristocrats could be found among its adherents.

Mozart's resignation from the service of the Archbishop of Salzburg,
at the age of twenty-five, was a historic declaration of artistic independence. Although this dignitary described Mozart as a "conceited
scoundrel" and Mozart referred to the archbishop in turn as a "pre-
sumptuous ecclesiastic",[5] the clash was not so much one of personalities
as of two worlds of culture. To the archbishop, who was one of the
powerful princes of the Holy Roman Empire, music was still feudal
and a musician belonged on the level of a footman or table waiter.
Mozart saw himself as something more, an artist, thinker, and human
being with human rights. As a free agent, however, his privations were
great and probably helped to cause his early death. It was not that he
failed to be appreciated or "understood" in his time. The fact was that,
like practically every great artist, his work was very much loved and
appreciated. Practically every musician in Austria and Germany knew
him as one of the great men, and tunes from his operas became the
rage, sung in the streets and arranged as beer-garden dances. "Figaro's
songs resounded in the streets and gardens, and even the harpist at the
Bierbank had to strike up *Non piu andrai* if he wanted people to
listen."[6] But a revolution was necessary before an artist could be
supported by a public. Mozart, for all the popularity of his music, still
had to seek the favor of penny-pinching kings and nobles, or of the
court lackeys who ran the backdoor politics of the opera houses. Typical
lines from his letters are: "The Queen wants to hear me play on
Tuesday, but I shan't make much money."[7] "My concert [in honor of
the coronation of Emperor Leopold II—*S.F.*] . . . was a splendid success from the point of view of honor and glory, but a failure as far as
money was concerned."[8] Critics as usual took the tone of their writings
from the aristocrats and snobs. They complained that Mozart offered
"too many beauties," or in other words that his music was more than

a light background for salon chatter. "He gives his hearers no time to breathe: as soon as one beautiful idea is grasped, it is succeeded by another, which drives the first from the mind: and so it goes on, until at the end, not one of these beauties remain in the memory." It never occurred to them that they might take a piece of music as a serious work of art.

Compared to Haydn's, Mozart's music has on the surface more of the mannerisms of the feudal world. Within this "galant" shell, however, it discloses even more poignant and anguished feelings. As in the case of Bach, there was no way in which he could address multitudes, and his more probing portrayals of emotional strife took the form of private expressions, over the heads of his customary audiences. No other composer could use so few notes to say so much, but only for those with ears to hear. Like Bach he had the entire "solar system" of the major-minor harmonic scheme at his fingertips, and there are passages where, for comic purposes or for especially deep expressions of pain, he foreshadows the practices of the contemporary "atonalists." Unlike the moderns, of course, he never makes a system or world view out of these extremes of dissonance and tension. It is out of obedience to feudal methods of music production that the form of the concerto for solo piano and orchestra holds so large a place in his output. This is not to imply that the concerto form has become outmoded since the eighteenth century. It played a powerful role in nineteenth-century music and is an important form today. Its preponderance in Mozart's output, however, indicates that in the musical circles for which he worked, the separation of composer and performer was not yet acknowledged. The composer still had to show off his talents as a public entertainer and "music-maker," like the improvising "poet-singers" of ancient societies. And so these concertos, most of them written for his own performance, were the form in which Mozart appeared as a musician before the nobility from whom he had to seek favors. They are, of course, works of the greatest beauty, in which he solved triumphantly the difficult problem of appearing to offer light entertainment, and yet providing a far deeper emotional undercurrent for those with open ears and mind. Also typical of the feudal attitude that still persisted in music was the fact that one of his last great works, the unfinished *Requiem,* was written for a count who, it later turned out, planned to offer the work as his own composition. After all, he had paid for it.

It is in the operas written during the last ten years of his life that Mozart expressed the full depth of his anti-feudal thinking, within a formal framework supplied by feudal culture. He abandoned poetic and "serious" opera, given over to the dream life of noble personages in a static and timeless world, and turned to comedy where, like the folk, he could express political thoughts under the mask of a buffoon. A remarkable characteristic of these comedies is that each one is a masterpiece of a wholly different comic style. *The Abduction from the Seraglio* was a popular romantic comedy telling of a maiden's rescue by her lover from a Turkish harem. There is much pointed dialogue in it about the independence of women, and in fact the women in it are given the most profound musical characterization, in dramatic and stormy arias. The opera was, moreover, a German-language work, written as such at a time when to be a patriot, and to advocate a national art understandable to the people, was to be pointedly political and anti-feudal. *Don Giovanni* adapted an ancient pattern of folk legend, the lionizing of the outlaw and sinner who is dragged down to Hell, but remains unrepentant and defiant to the very end. "The devil" gets the best music, and in fact the heroic music that Mozart gives to the Don, emphasizing his defiance of social convention, leads directly to Beethoven. With *The Marriage of Figaro* Mozart moved from symbolic to realistic comedy. As in *Don Giovanni* there is a lecherous nobleman and a comic servant. But they are no longer stock myth characters, from no particular time or place. A light of contemporary reality is thrown about the situations, with the Count exposed as a hypocrite and fool. The servant, Figaro, is no longer the stereotype buffoon, like Don Giovanni's Leporello, but the hero of the piece, fully realized in music as a human being, fighting for his right to love and winning. Figaro's air, *"Non piu andrai,"* which swept all Vienna, satirized the army at a time when young men were being dragged to fight Austrian imperial wars. The women in this opera are likewise most profound characterizations, the Countess being depicted as a victim of feudal double standards, and the servant, Susanna, emerging as the wisest person of all. *The Magic Flute* was Mozart's second German-language work and in fact may be called the first "people's opera," not spon-

sored by the courts at all but put on as a popular commercial entertainment. On the surface, its story is a fairy-tale fantasy full of comic
vaudeville, but it is actually open praise of the Masonic order, emphasizing its ideals of humanitarianism and contempt for rank and title with
Mozart's grandest and most sublime music. An obvious symbolism in
the work was the rich use by Mozart, a Catholic, of the old German
Lutheran chorales, with their national-patriotic connotations. The part
of the clown, Papageno, was played by the producer himself, Schikaneder, and it contained many barbs pointed at "princes," some in the
libretto and even more ad-libbed. This work, contrary to the myth
that Mozart was not understood by his times, was an immense success,
and precisely among the common people of the city. Finally *Cosi Fan
Tutti,* opening with the tone of an airy comedy of manners, described
with the most subtle and entrancing music the transition in two women
from the youthful game of puppy love to the deeper passions of
maturity.

The fact that in all of these comedies except *The Marriage of
Figaro,* which was threatened with censorship, Mozart had to use feudal
symbolism for anti-feudal ideas, has allowed these works to be misinterpreted in later times. It is characteristic of the myth patterns of
feudalism, both the upper class tales of chivalry and the peasant folklore,
that in an age of bourgeois realism they are taken as material for children. To see them this way is, of course, to misunderstand them. Yet
the fact that such symbolism had to be used by even the most progressive minds was a real limitation, not only upon the form but upon the
ideas that could be expressed within that form. Mozart was the last
great composer to suffer from the disparity between depth of thought
and feeling, on the one hand, and the outer forms forced by feudalism
upon the greatest minds that rose within it. These grotesqueries were
swept away by the French Revolution of 1789, which transformed the
cultural world along with the social and political, not only in France
but throughout Europe. In this new world Mozart's music—thoroughly
misinterpreted—was used by feudal-minded critics as the standard of
"correctness" to chastise such ground-breaking realists as Beethoven
and Schubert.

4. *"Pure Music" and Social Conflict*

LUDWIG VAN BEETHOVEN (1770-1827) was nineteen years old when the French Revolution broke out. It may seem contradictory that the greatest musical expression of the ideas born of the French Revolution should have come from a man who was born in Germany and spent most of his life in Vienna. The revolution, however, was a world event. For a few years there ruled a government based on the declaration of the "Rights of Man," universal male suffrage, the separation of Church and State. The peasants and working people of France, whose uprising had touched off the revolution, beat back the armies of feudal reaction led by German and Austrian princes. True, the middle class, having gained the power they sought, turned savagely against the left, wiping out most of the democratic gains and laying the basis for the dictatorship of Napoleon. But this dictatorship was a façade for the rule not of a landed nobility, but of the great bankers and industrialists. Distinctions of "birth" were swept away. The new ruling class were owners of factories, stocks, bonds, and money capital. Market-place competition became the form of the "new freedom," and the masses of people, uprooted from the land, were likewise "free" to offer their labor and talents in the market place.

This cataclysm shook all Europe. The best feudal armies were being trounced by the French working people singing the "Marseillaise," and by the "upstart" corporal, Napoleon. In order to save themselves, the princes had to draw, however guardedly, upon the national liberation sentiments of the common people. An example of the impact of these developments upon tsarist Russia, for example, is given by the great Russian critic, Vissarion Belinsky (1811-1848). "On the one hand the year 1812, which shook the whole of Russia from end to end, roused her dormant forces and revealed to her hitherto unsuspected wells of strength; it welded, by a sense of common danger, all the diffused interests of private wills, blunted through national desuetude, into a single huge mass, stirred up the national consciousness and national pride, and in this way fostered the birth of publicity as the precursor of public opinion; furthermore the year 1812 inflicted a telling blow on petrified usage; it witnessed the disappearance of the non-serving nobles, who peacefully came into the world and peacefully went out of it in their country places, beyond whose sacred precincts they never ventured; the backwoods swiftly disappeared together with the staggering survivals of ancient usage."[1] The partisan movement of the peasantry against the invaders grew into demands for land and for the abolition of serfdom. In central Europe the revolution inspired national patriotic movements and demands for constitutional government.

Beethoven was born in the city of Bonn, on the Rhine. His father was a badly paid court musician, and his mother the widow of a cook. The Rhineland, adjacent to France, was deeply stirred by the events across the border, and as a young musician in the court orchestra of the Elector of Cologne, Beethoven learned much of the exciting popular revolutionary music of France. The Vienna which he entered in 1792 to make his permanent home, was alive with middle class democratic sentiment, which took the form of a deep interest in anything that spoke for "freedom" in the arts and hinted at the overthrow of old institutions. Napoleon's declaration of himself as emperor, and his control over the German principalities, smashed the hollow shell of the Holy Roman Empire, a relic of the Middle Ages. In answer, Austria declared itself an independent empire. Each emperor in turn promised "reforms," none of which was actually forthcoming. In this atmosphere it was possible for Beethoven to win support for his revolutionary music, even among some liberal and music-loving nobles. Nevertheless, it took great courage for him to proclaim his pro-French and republican sentiments, while in the name of these sentiments Austrian imperial armies were being beaten. He dedicated his great Third Symphony, the "Heroic" or "Eroica," to Napoleon, and made his republican feelings even more obvious when he tore the dedication up after Napoleon became emperor in 1804.

Beethoven's music falls into three periods, as scholars have traditionally described it. In the first he was still a young man making his way
as a musician, giving lessons to the wealthy and performing at their
private concerts. He wrote a number of piano sonatas and chamber
music works which still preserve in their outer form the feudal character of music for the salons and the well-off amateurs, although these
works have a boisterousness and rugged dramatic power which takes
them far outside the bounds of light entertainment.

In his second period, from about 1802 to 1814, Beethoven was able
to realize both in his way of life and in the form and content of his
music what was essentially a new world view. He lived differently from
all earlier composers except Handel, who had been his own manager
in England. He walked among the nobles as their equal and superior.
He accepted commissions for works but wrote them as he pleased.
He made his major income from the publication and sale of his music,
and from concerts open to the mass public. Contrary to the myth that
he was "ahead" of his times, his works, eagerly bid for by publishers,
made him famous throughout Germany, France, England, Russia, and
even the young United States. He was granted a pension by three
Viennese noblemen when it was feared that he would leave Vienna,
but he wore nobody's livery and was nobody's servant. Some biographers
show a squeamishness about his dealings in money matters, as if it
were not fitting for an artist to drive a bargain. But in moving from
feudal patronage to the market place, Beethoven had to handle the
market place on its own hard terms.

Musically, this is the period of his major symphonies, from the
Second through the Eighth, of the opera, *Fidelio,* the violin concerto,
the last three piano concertos, dramatic overtures written for the
theater such as "Egmont" and "Coriolanus," and a number of string
quartets and piano sonatas which gave a new dramatic and emotional
richness to these traditional "salon" and "amateur" forms. The symphonies affirmed the central place of the public concert hall in musical
life. The public concert, which had been growing in the eighteenth
century as an occasional and secondary avenue of musical performance,
now became the major arena where reputations were made, the forum
where the middle class came to hear new and challenging works. The
movement of instrumental music out of the feudal salons to the theaters,

where the middle class could become its sponsors, was a revolutionary step, and the concert hall contained this electric atmosphere. The public production of the symphonies themselves was a social act. It was made possible not only by the ticket-buying public but by the musicians themselves who, making their living in labor for the aristocracy and church, offered their services in a symphony because they were genuinely interested in hearing and fostering this music. An anecdote tells of Beethoven's brusqueness with a faltering clarinet player, which so offended the other members of the orchestra that they vowed never to play for Beethoven again. "But this lasted only until he came forward with a new composition, when the curiosity of the musicians got the better of their anger."[2]

The symphonies of this period are public orations in the greatest sense of the term, and a similar tone of heroic public address characterizes all the other works of the period. What is not so commonly recognized, in the present day of formalistic criticism, when the simplest song is "analyzed" so that it emerges as an inexplicable puzzle, is how truly popular these symphonies were, in intent and effect. Both Beethoven and his audiences looked upon the symphony as a popularization of music, and in fact the more refined critics thought of it as vulgar. The idiom he started with was that of folk and popular dance, march and song. The third Symphony has a funeral march, and a march in its last movement. The Fourth and Sixth Symphonies are suffused with folk music. The Fifth Symphony is full of marches and processionals, as in the great coda of the first movement and the opening of the last movement. The Seventh Symphony has been rightly called the "apotheosis of the dance." The Eighth is a masterpiece of humor, teasing the listeners with seemingly bizarre harmonic and rhythmic twists. There is no contradiction between this and the fact that these works rank with the most profound in the history of music. One may compare them to the work of a novelist who starts with characters who are recognized by the readers as typical, realistic, and familiar. From this point on he can take them through the most profound and illuminating patterns of life and conflict. The demands of both popularity and realism have been met, however, by the common ground of real life and people between artist and audience. So Beethoven was both popular and understood; at the same time he gave harmonic and structural ideas to composers for the next century. It may seem strange to commentators today, feeling that they have "discovered" Beethoven through their technical analyses, that Beethoven was understood in his own times better than today. But he was, and he wanted to be understood. He had no compunction about giving titles to his works, letting it be known for instance that his "Eroica" Symphony dealt with a heroic leader of the people, and pointedly using in the last movement a theme he had once associated with Prometheus, the revolutionist among the Greek myth gods. His one opera, *Fidelio*, was a typical "rescue" melodrama, such as had been popular in Paris during the revolution, and was written in "comic" style, meaning not flippant, of course, but popular, with the vernacular language, spoken dialogue, and melodious airs. Much is made in later commentaries of the attacks upon Beethoven by the music critics, but they did not represent the public. They were the "educated" writers, subservient to the witch-hunting press for which they worked, serving the most reactionary forces in Viennese life. As is always the way with reactionary critics, who recognize the cultural threat to their patrons, they try to destroy the new realism by accusing the work of poor craft, bad taste, ignorance of the correct rules, vulgarity. Yet even they had to recognize Beethoven as a "genius" who seemed to be "going wild." The people—meaning of course the city middle class, for the great exploited working population on the land could not be reached by even the greatest of bourgeois realists—flocked to his concerts. He was the idol of all forward-looking and progressive minds. His friend and first biographer, Schindler, writes of his "never ceasing opposition to every existing political institution"[3] and says that "in his political sentiments Beethoven was a republican."[4] The pianist Moscheles writes of how, in 1804, his teacher warned him against the "eccentricities" of Beethoven, whereupon Moscheles sought out a Beethoven sonata and from that time on "seized upon the piano-forte works of Beethoven as they successively appeared and in them found a solace and delight such as no other composer afforded me."[5]

The third period, from about 1814 to Beethoven's death, has been made into something of a mystery. After the outpouring of the great stream of symphonic works, there is a lapse of eleven years, from 1812 to 1823, in which no symphony appears, and after that only one

—the tremendous Ninth. It is the period of the great last piano sonatas and string quartets. The fundamental reason for this change lies in the events following the defeat of Napoleon. The "tyrant" had been defeated, but on the heels of this came the worst tide of political reaction, the restoration of feudal despots on every throne, and the attempt of the Council of Vienna and the Holy Alliance to stamp out democratic movements wherever they showed themselves, even as far off as the Americas. The atmosphere of Vienna was thick with police spying and clerical-political censorship of every spoken and written word. Peoples who had fought Napoleon and been given promises of reform were savagely repressed. Under such conditions a further stream of public democratic orations in music was inconceivable, and Beethoven turned to the more intimate forms of the piano sonata and string quartet. He gave these works, however, the scope and grandeur of his greatest symphonies. They had nothing of the salon atmosphere that had once characterized these forms, but were a "musicians' music," speaking to the "few" at a time when a mass public could not be reached. They are deeply introspective and subjective, among the most poignant works ever written. Even here, however, there is no surrender to despair, but always the sense of struggle which may be called the keynote of Beethoven's character, and always a final serenity and affirmation of faith in life.

When Beethoven worked out his Ninth Symphony, it was as if he felt that in this new Vienna, the electric democratic atmosphere no longer existed in the concert hall, and without this base, the social meaning of the "pure" symphony, as he had once conceived it, would no longer be understood. And so he set its last movement to the words of Schiller's "Ode to Joy" and praise of human brotherhood. He wrote this entire movement in the popular style of the choruses from *Fidelio,* and created as its main melody a broad swinging tune of the kind that could catch the mind and be sung by people almost on its first hearing. Another work of this period, the great *Missa Solemnis,* although set to the words of the Mass, was anything but church music, and the dramatic, proclamatory music sung by the chorus to the words *"Dona nobis pacem,"* a cry for peace in the midst of military sounds, could leave no doubt in the listener's minds as to the message of the work. It was during this late period that the poet Grillparzer wrote in the deaf Beethoven's conversation book, "Musicians after all cannot be affected by the censorship; if they only knew what you think when you write your music!"[6]

Later commentators have not been so clear. In typical romantic style, they accept Beethoven's heroism but abstract it from real struggles, making it a kind of individual "defiance of society" exhibited by his deliberately throwing "dissonances" and "new chords" in the face of an audience that presumably wanted only sweet sounds. The central character of Beethoven's forms, however, is their realism, rising to the demands of the times. Musical realism does not consist, of course, of the imitation of wind, water, bird calls, and the other sounds of nature, although these may have a legitimate place in a composer's over-all conception. Beethoven's realism shows itself in many ways. One is the understandable human imagery of his melodies and themes, a social product of the musical life of his times. Another is his mastery of the new stage of development of music, the possibilities of the magnificent collective instrument of the symphony orchestra and the possibilities of the public concert hall. In the great Beethoven symphonic works, everything is addressed to the listener's ear, boldly and openly said, meant to be heard. The counterpoint is always clear to the ear and dramatically justified. The bold harmonic flights and dissonances are not made into a "system," a "value" in themselves, as they became to some pettier later minds, but they are always psychologically justified. The pain, anguish, tension, or fantastic humor they convey is always resolved on a new level of acceptance of reality. The most important aspect of Beethoven's realism is that the over-all organization of his music is guided by nothing other than the movement, dramatic action, conflict, and resolution of real life, as seen by a great social mind who had understood the social conflicts of his day, taken a part in fighting them through, and brought clarity of understanding to experience.

The general name given to Beethoven's type of musical organization, as seen in his symphonies, sonatas, and chamber music, is "sonata form," which may be freely defined as an instrumental music which embodies its own dramatic life. Themes or subjects are introduced in what is established as the basic key or tonality. They are developed rhythmically and harmonically, with a sense of the movement away from the opening and the piling up of tension and conflict, and then are resolved, returning to the opening tonality, but with the themes now seen in a transformed light. Certain patterns or rules have been advanced in schools as to the "proper" way to construct a work in sonata form. But in Beethoven's works, and in all great handling of sonata form, there is really no guide for each step in the music but real life itself, as the artist has lived it and reflects it in the music. Each step in change of mood or emotion, each conflict and resolution, must seem real and convincing. Thus the music reflects and awakens a similar life in the listener. Beethoven's music moves continually through a series of dramatic oppositions. One theme or musical phrase is answered by another contrasting one. A passage in one rhythm is answered by a passage in another. A dissonance, impelling to further movement, is answered by a consonance, or halting place. Passages in the high notes are answered by passages in the bass, solo instrumental voices are answered by massed sound, one tonality is answered by another. It is a kind of music written to fit the instruments, exploring their full possibilities, and yet made possible only by the long development of song, operatic and dramatic music preceding it. Passages which are in obvious song or dance style, sometimes even a kind of "aria," alternate with what are obviously "recitative" passages, full of speech inflections. The movement of a theme or subject through a series of harmonic transformations has the aspect of a gigantic recitative, or inner monologue, resolved again in passages of a powerful rhythmic and song character. The end of a work is a summation and resolution of conflicts, so that it is not conflict itself which is the goal but the ability to work through it, thus to arrive at an ending with clarity, assurance, and renewed strength. And so this music does not merely reflect the feelings of the listeners but transforms them through the composer's thought, giving them an aroused consciousness of the historic social movement of which they are a part. Such realistic music makes new demands upon the composer's art. A major work sums up a long process of struggle and thought, and by the same token, it cannot be repeated in content and form. The composer must then advance to new problems, wrestle with them and solve them.

What are the ideas contained in Beethoven's music? We can answer this when we see that ideas do not consist of things, such as persons or trees, or of emotions, such as joy, yearning, sorrow. Ideas are relationships between things, as reflected in the mind of a person who is touching, moving among, and living among these things. Social ideas are relationships among people, as seen by one who takes a part in and shares the historical movements and struggles in which people are involved. These ideas are accompanied by emotions, which is nothing more than a sign of the fact that it is a living human being who is thus examining and expressing his relationships to nature and to people. The presence of emotion is a sign that the relations are human, not mechanistic. There is no valid thought without feeling, no valid idea without emotion, or in other words without application to life. Emotions are engendered by real acts and real experiences. Those who claim that they express no emotions in art, or that the emotions are a product of the "unconscious," demonstrate not a "clear-headed" or "scientific" spirit, but dehumanization in the one case, impotence in the other.

Thus we can discover the ideas contained in Beethoven's works by relating the emotions of the works to the social realities of the time which engendered them. In other words, we must ask ourselves what these emotions are about. The fundamental reality was the cracking of feudalism, the victories of bourgeois democracy, the freeing of the individual from feudal servitude. Had a composer then consistently written music that was light, refined, and gay, in the aristocratic dance and salon forms, the ideas expressed would have been those of flight from the storms of life, the attempt to recover a tight, static little feudal world untouched by time or reality, to make believe that nothing was happening. Had a composer consistently written music that was a long, unbroken lamentation, the ideas would have been those of despair at the passing of the old world. But Beethoven filled his symphonic works with stormy emotional conflicts, displaying his recognition of a world that was itself in process of violent conflict and rapid change. He expressed deeply sorrowful and tragic feelings, recognizing the casualties of the struggle for progress. He resolved all of these feelings in an expression of overwhelming joy and triumph, indicating his feeling that change was good, and through it humanity was discovering new powers of life and development. The conscious social thinking at the base of this music is confirmed by the fact that

Beethoven chose so public an arena for its presentation, where he could speak to the rising middle class. And the effect of his music on the times was to provide a rallying point, a sense of common experience and kinship, for all anti-feudal minds, for all who welcomed the conflicts of their time and found progress in them.

Why has all this been deliberately obscured? As capitalism was assured of its victory over feudalism, and as the working class grew, organized, and educated itself, the study of the anti-feudal revolutions was frowned upon by the ruling class. The great artists who reflected and helped fight out this movement in the realm of ideas, were transformed into mythical personages, whose achievements were seen as vague flickerings of a misty "genius" or simply as the invention of technical improvements in the art. Beethoven's sonatas were widely performed and enjoyed in his lifetime; his symphonies were acclaimed; his Ninth Symphony and last quartets, considered "abstruse" to this day, were performed without trouble and with evident public appreciation in his time. When he died, all Vienna turned out for his funeral. But it is true that a generation or two later, the great mass of his works had to be "rediscovered" and fought for, and that process is continuing to this day. It came to be fondly assumed that Beethoven's own public was blind, and that in some mysterious way he had addressed only "posterity."

Certainly Beethoven's music is not devoid of personal feelings. But there is no barrier in art between the personal and the social. A change in social and political institutions brings a new kind of personality to the forefront of history, which it is the task of art to disclose. If we take Beethoven's music simply as a portrayal of a human mind—and it is far more than that—it is the portrayal of a mind wholly conscious of life, reacting to every event with the utmost sensitivity and depth of feeling, boldly rejecting whatever it saw to be useless and outmoded, the kind of mind that in political life was then in the forefront of history and was declaring the "Rights of Man." The expressions of love which may be found in the "Moonlight" and "Appassionata" piano sonatas, or in Fidelio, have a mixture of tenderness and joy, of unrest resolving in a full acceptance of life, far different from the feudal game of love-making, with its sentimentality and mock self-pity. They are far different as well from the erotic blind obsessions and self-destruction that Wagner was to portray in music two generations later. The beautiful slow movement of Beethoven's First String Quartet, which he himself described as the tomb scene from *Romeo and Juliet,* describes not the acceptance of death but the struggle for life, and the great "Eroica" funeral march is not merely lamenting but grand and heroic, with a powerful struggle at its center. The "personal" in Beethoven is the personality of a social and revolutionary mind.

Also assisting at the mystification of Beethoven's art, and in fact of all art, is the theory, popular among the self-styled "scientific" critics of today, that "thought" must be separated from "feeling." Things are presumed to be seen clearly only when they are divested of emotions, or in other words removed from their human relationships; and emotions are properly felt only if they are divested of the things that engendered them, or in other words felt as the mysterious forces of the "unconscious." The result of course is no scientific clarity, but only a dehumanization of objects, so that music is created as if it consisted of little puzzles of sound patterns, and emotions are treated as if they were inexplicable apparitions, a separate aspect of art to which the composer gives birth as if he were an unconscious automaton. The contemporary concert hall has also fostered the separation of music from life, feeling from thought, emotions from objects. It is no longer an arena for the battling out of contemporary ideas and concepts of life in music. The great works of the past are accordingly presented as a kind of escape from the present. The grander and more heroic the past conflicts, the more successful the escape, like a historical novel in which wars and sword-play appear so glamorously different from wars today.

Finally another set of misconceptions rises out of the fact that Beethoven's revolutionary achievement took the form of apparently "pure" music, without word, story, or stage action: the orchestral symphony, piano sonata, and string quartet. This has fostered the belief that thenceforth the "true course" of music had to be in "purity." But this seeming "purity" of Beethoven's music, which does not hold true even in his case, considering his overtures and vocal works, is a product of the fact that in past class society progress often had to take place in a one-sided way. Beethoven's choice of forms was conditioned by the censorship and clerical atmosphere that hung heavy over Vienna. The question of realism could not be fought out in church music or the music of feudal-controlled opera, the only other large architectural forms of the time. Thus the symphony as he developed it became a form capable of broad content, rich experience, and stirring drama, free from the manacles of church ritual and the feudalisms that still infested the opera house. This communication was possible in wordless forms because the audiences understood clearly just what this move to the concert hall represented. The effect of Beethoven's great realisms was not to make music "pure" but to sweep the archaic out of all forms of music. Their liberating effect is seen not only in the tradition of concert symphony and sonata that follows him, but in every kind of music that arises after him, which must follow or seem to follow in its organization and content the movement and flow of life and the portrayal of a rounded human mind.

Beethoven's art is the classic creation of bourgeois realism in music, and it exhibits both the great qualities and limitations of bourgeois realism. In its middle class audiences, which are so much larger than the audiences of feudal music, and yet so small compared to the real population of the country, it reflects the fact that the great cultural achievements of capitalism, like its economic progress, take place in the cities at the expense of the countryside. It is a social music, possible only to a profoundly socially conscious and forward-looking mind. Yet in its tendency to portray social movements predominantly in terms of a heroic individual psychology, which seems to stand apart from society, in its overemphasis on wordlessness and its occasional use of mystical imagery, it indicates that the most progressive bourgeois minds raised questions of freedom and progress which they could not solve in a realistic and practical way. Its exaltation of the public concert hall as the primary center of great musical experience, and its exaltation of a professional music at the expense of music for amateur participation, were necessary progressive steps. Yet they were also narrowing steps, which could lead to a destructive one-sidedness of music unless further revolutionary achievements were to make music truly popular, addressed to all the people and participated in by them, in a way that in Beethoven's time was impossible.

5. *Art For Art's Sake and the Philistines*

ALL NINETEENTH CENTURY economic, political and social life was stirred into movement by the destruction of feudalism in France. But new contradictions appeared. To the working class there was no freedom, not even that of suffrage, for even parliamentary democracy demanded property qualifications for the vote. To live, the worker had to sell his labor power in competition with growing numbers of unemployed. To whatever job he moved, he found himself faced with the same conditions, a bare subsistence pay at best, and the constant menace of starvation. And so, against the most brutal suppression, independent organizations began to grow among the working class. These took such forms as trade unions in England and France, the Chartist movement in England, socialist groups in France, a revolt of the Silesian weavers in Germany. The middle class of small business men, traders, and shopkeepers, the class which had felt most completely "liberated" by the break-up of feudalism, found itself afflicted by contradictions as mysterious to it as they were oppressive. In 1825 appeared the first of what was to be a periodic series of economic crises, from which the large bankers and industrialists emerged richer and stronger. In 1830 revolution broke out in France, supported by almost the entire population, but resulting only in replacing one king with another who was backed by a somewhat broader oligarchy of bankers and factory owners. Then in 1848, following another economic crisis, a revolutionary movement swept France, Germany, Austria, and Italy.

In the realm of the production of music, the "freedom" of the market place, which actually amounted to the printing of music for public sale and the offering of public concerts, showed similar contradictions. To Beethoven and his audiences, the break from aristocratic patronage into the "free market" had been a great step of liberation.

But by the 1820's, the same publishers who begged Beethoven for new works had become a power on the market. To them music was nothing more than a commodity, manufactured for sale. Far preferable to the idiosyncracies of a "genius" was the standardized work produced by a musical hack, who could turn out streams of imitation folk music, or superficial borrowings from the great revolutionary realistic music, reduced to some easily digested form. This is the basic pattern of the mass-produced "popular music" of bourgeois society, which is anything but "of the people." It represents both the huckster's fear and hatred of anything really new and a frantic search for "novelty," a parasitical feeding upon the great music produced during the heroic period of the rise of the nation.

Franz Schubert (1797-1828) grew to maturity in a Vienna where Beethoven was still alive and idolized, but publishers were not interested in any new "genius." The son of a poverty-stricken school teacher, Schubert attempted to make a living out of music. He lived in poverty, but not because he was, as the romantic myth puts it, "ahead of his times," an "enigma" to the "common herd." During his lifetime his songs became the rage in Viennese homes. But he was given the most meager pay by publishers. The critics, as usual, fulfilled their function as unofficial cultural police agents by putting a finger of disapproval on what was precisely his ground-breaking achievement—the rich use of Austrian folk song and dance as materials for the most deeply emotional, dramatic, and exalted composition. Thus a review of one of his stage works complains: "The music for *The Twin Brothers* has much originality and many interesting passages, and the declamation is correct; but it is a blot upon the work that the sentiments of simple country folk are interpreted much too seriously, not to say heavy-handedly, for a comic subject. . . . Comic music, it seems to us, does not take at all kindly to a very close adherence to the words, or to the composer's taking refuge in a modulation whenever pain, for instance, is mentioned."[1] To this feudal mind, any entrance of the village folk or peasantry, on stage or through their characteristic music, must necessarily be "comic." A reviewer of a different work writes: "The introduction to the third act, by the way, is so like dance music that one is scarcely able to conceal one's astonishment, although the piece is otherwise quite pretty."[2] The images created by Schubert's songs and instrumental works declare precisely that the "simple country folk" are no longer to be seen as clowns, but as human beings with their right to love and sorrow.

It was the Vienna of after 1815, where Metternich and the reactionary Holy Alliance tried to set up a world-wide witch-hunt against democratic beliefs. Student friends of Schubert were arrested by the police. Schubert, so great a master of vocal music, never wrote a successful stage work, the obvious reason being that he could not get a worthwhile libretto, for the stage was heavily censored. All plays had to be submitted to the police, and the writer was lucky if he got a reply in five years. Schubert had the intellect to set works of Goethe, Schiller, and Heine to music with the deepest insight, the latter poet requiring courage as well. The stifling reactionary, clerical, and imperial atmosphere continued unbroken until 1848, and without much break indeed until the twentieth century. It was effective not only in its direct censorship, but in the sheer ignorance of everything social, political, and historical which it forced upon all minds brought up under it.

"Romanticism" is a general name often given to the whole of the arts of the revolutionary period, including in its sweep the great realistic achievements. It is a product, however, not only of revolution but also of censorship and counter-revolution. "Romantic" tendencies showed themselves before 1789 as a kind of vague dissatisfaction with the tight aristocratic and church patterns forced upon the arts. It took such forms as a turn to the idealization of the "simple folk," an interest in the early art of the Middle Ages and the "Gothic," where folk craftsmanship took seemingly mysterious, yet harrowing religious and primitive forms, a turn to "nature" as a backdrop for the "man alone," an interest in everything strange, exotic, and magical, even a Catholic revival. It is true that many of the great anti-feudal realists, such as Beethoven, had something of the visionary romantic about them, as if they could not quite see the real and practical paths to the freedom and progress which they so genuinely proclaimed. But the sweep of romanticism after 1830 was increasingly influenced by the tide of reaction, in which the great bankers and industrialists were consolidating their power and were everywhere fearful of the forces that had been unleashed among the common people, the peasantry and working class. Romanticism then took such forms as deep yearnings for "free-

dom," which seek the path to freedom everywhere but in the real
world, and so express these yearnings in the strange and the exotic or
attach them to subjects that cannot adequately contain such feelings.
And so the subjects become "symbolic," like a grasped straw or a
transitory means to express the "inexplicable." Romanticism may be
seen in Schubert in the tragic feelings of such song cycles as "The
Maid of the Mill" and "The Winter Journey," which are not adequately
explained by the sentimental and shallow story of the heart-broken,
jilted, and wandering lover. What they reveal is a deep unrest in
Schubert, and in the Austrian people for whom he felt so deep an attach-
ment and sympathy. Also romantic are the sudden outbreaks of passion in his instrumental works; they flare up in the midst of the most
charming passages and as suddenly subside. Yet at the core of Schubert's
strength is his realistic quality, seen in the earthy human imagery of
his melody, so full of the presence of people and of genuine joy in
life. These qualities made him seem "vulgar" to the critics of the time.

Beethoven near the end of his life had noticed that his music,
at first so well understood, was no longer being understood or performed correctly. "A certain class of piano-forte performers seemed to
lose intelligence and feeling in proportion as they gained dexterity of
fingering." Not only was the playing too fast, but it was also too loud.
Orchestral performances were coming to be places in which "noise was
paramount."[3] The concert hall was losing its character as an anti-feudal
arena of new ideas, and was becoming a place in which the newly
risen wealthy could show that they were as "cultured" as the feudal
nobility, and as little interested in the real world. The difference was
that now unreality had to be expressed in the terms which had accompanied the rise of this class to power, the seeming bigness of
proclamation and air of heroic conflict. The concert hall also began to
take on the limitations of a business enterprise. Its managers found
it easier to advertise, sell, and profit from a glamorous soloist-personality
performing sure-fire music than to enter the world of disturbing ideas
and arguments. To Beethoven bigness of sound had been a quality
to handle respectfully and only when the bigness of his thought
demanded this kind of public oration. But now bigness was demanded
of all music, however thin its real content. Everything must appear
to be heroic in attitude, unreal and misty in subject.

The meaning of the great progressive step of separating the composer from the public performer, quickly became dissipated. The composer was "freed" of the necessity to entertain an audience through his technique and improvisations, but this "freedom" took on the aspect of a prison. The "virtuoso" of the piano and violin, the purveyor of big sounds and bravura effects, became the reigning monarch of the musical world, far outstripping the composer in monetary return, offering the audiences a seemingly heroic ritual in which musical sounds—their content hardly mattered—were recreated before their eyes by the sweat and strain of the human body. The Italian violinist, Niccolo Paganini (1784-1840), would cut three strings of his violin before the audience to show the feats he could perform on the fourth alone. A typical program of Franz Liszt (1811-1886), the first of the great concert pianists, was top-heavy with "fantasias" on airs from popular operas of the day, as if the performer were recreating on the piano all the dazzling virtuoso sounds of an orchestra and singers combined.

Paganini and Liszt were composers of very great talent. Liszt particularly was prolific in what seemed to be startlingly new ideas of musical sound and texture—the "symphonic poem," which proclaimed its break with the "pure music" of the past; the impressionist piano piece, devoted to the sights and sounds of nature; the one-movement concerto; works such as the Hungarian Rhapsodies, which openly proclaimed their national spirit. All of these "innovations" could have been found, with less fanfare about them, in some of the work of older masters, like Beethoven and Schubert. Liszt may be called the first of the "modernists," who extract one element from the rounded body of realistic music and consider it a new invention. Beethoven's "innovation," that everything in a concert piece must be understandable to the listener, was vulgarized by making everything transparent and sensational. Every musical theme, whether a folk song or a melodious sigh, had to be dressed up in heroic sound. The concerto for solo pianist or violinist and orchestra became a kind of imitation symphony or symphonic poem in which the great emotional conflicts of a Beethoven work were replaced by a mighty battle of sounds between the soloist and the orchestra.

The strength of the piano music of Frederick Chopin (1810-1849) came from the melodic idiom he had learned from the songs and dances of his native Poland. This idiom suffuses not only his pieces with dance titles, like the Mazurkas and Polonaises, but all his other works, his Nocturnes, Ballades, Concertos. His music had the romantic character of a "song without words," and so the fervent national patriotic feeling, which he expressed with such fire and tenderness, seemed to come not from the outside world but "from within the heart." Yet through his art the idiom of Polish national music became part of world art, and at the same time his works became a beloved national heritage of the people of his native land. He transformed the technique of writing for and performing on the piano by making the instrument "sing" as it had never done before. Yet in its very popularity as a kind of "cosmopolitan" concert piano music, the national qualities of his music were vitiated. A new kind of performance developed which offered improvisation in disguise, an improvisation consisting of "interpretations" of his and other composers' music, which was stretched and contracted like a rubber band to suit the performer's feelings of the moment. Critics began to blame the sensationalism of such performances—those of Paganini and Liszt, for example—upon the "mob," although the "mob" to which this music appealed consisted of the wealthy and titled people of Europe.

There were many musicians of great talent who genuinely worshiped the giants of the past, notably Beethoven, and tried to carry on the great tradition. But the bourgeois composers saw this achievement only as a musical one, not one fought out in social life as well. The two great functions of the composer were wrested from them, unless they fought for them. These two functions were the writing of songs and dances for the people to use, and the public presentation of ideas in musical experiences on a high epic, dramatic, and heroic level. Both of these functions had been taken over and distorted by the market place, the one becoming a factory industry and the other a kind of acrobatic circus. The bourgeois composer, however, tended to take this state of affairs, just as the bankrupt shopkeeper took the competition and crises that had destroyed him, as if it were mysteriously ordained for all time. The composer saw the publisher and concert manager as the "philistine." The whole world was full of "philistines." He looked upon even the common people as "philistines," although they were no more responsible for the adulteration of music than they were for the adulteration of bread. The artist was always destined to be a "misunderstood genius," always "ahead" of the public. Thus, issuing fiery manifestoes and brandishing his weapons, he departed from the real battlefield. The experiences he put into his music, accordingly, were his own subjective anguish and yearning; for he had lost touch with the popular and with the heroic and dramatic, or, in other words, with the real world. The art of music was divided in two, with each part half an art. On the one hand were the manufactured "popular" songs and dances and the concert display pieces, with their appearance of joy in life and extrovert display of the human powers. These appeared understandable and heroic, but were only a flimsy imitation of the great revolutionary song and symphonic art, like a calendar imitation of a Renaissance painting. Serious music on the other hand, drawing its strength from the great past achievements of harmony and seeking "true feelings," took the direction of flight from reality.

These early romantic composers include some of great creative power, a power which comes from the fact that they express human feelings of the sincerest kind, and even a frightening pain. But the mind portrayed in their music is less social, more introverted. Even their form disintegrates, for it is the past forms which they try to re-create with the added subjective "feelings" of the present. There is no longer in their music a fund of varied human images taken from the real world, but a constant probing of self and an attempt to resolve inner conflicts, which is always fruitless for their source is sought everywhere but in the realities that engendered them. They fight the philistinism of the market place in a way that is itself bourgeois, individualistic, competitive. A story related by the great French romantic, Hector Berlioz (1803-1869), indicates how deeply the market place commodity spirit ate into the composers. "It was during my rides in the neighborhood of Rome with Felix Mendelssohn [1809-1847] that I told him how surprised I was that no one had written a scherzo on Shakespeare's glittering little poem 'Queen Mab.' He was equally surprised, and I instantly regretted having put the idea into his head. For several years afterwards I dreaded hearing that he had carried it out."[4]

Berlioz regarded himself as a revolutionary in music. A friend, Hiller, writes of him, "He respected no one but Shakespeare, Goethe and Beethoven. He was at war with all conventions."[5] He lived as if he were surrounded by wolves. He tried to go "beyond" Beethoven in making his symphonic works even more monumental and splendid in sound, and adding to all of them stories, symbols, words, literary programs. And in his work we may see the weakness of the romantic "tone poem," or instrumental work to a literary title or story. The trouble is not with the idea of tone poems or "program music," as many purist critics find, but with the kind of story or "program" that is used, which often makes a work of this type more incomprehensible than a work of "pure music." The listener can relate every episode of the music to some story, but the question then arises: What does the story mean? Berlioz' literary themes are the typical unreal romantic symbols for a real unrest: the brigand, the corsair, the lonely wanderer, the opium dream, the suicidal lover, Faust and the Devil, the "Last Judgment." And his music, for all its emotional and melodic power, and for all its picturesque clothing, lacks the true drama found not only in Beethoven but also in the instrumental works of Haydn and Mozart—the creation of contrasting musical images in interplay with one another, the constant moving through a series of dramatic oppositions out of which music gets its forward motion.

Composers, withdrawing from social life, became one-sided in art. Robert Schumann (1810-1856) in Germany, who also tried to emulate Beethoven and go "further," wrote his finest music in small forms strung together. They have the air of a private diary which the audience was inadvertently reading. He thought about his music, as well as his critical writings, as if they were a product of two personalities warring within him. He gave these personalities the names of Florestan and Eusebius, one impetuous and the other dreamy. Thus conflict to him seemed to proceed not out of real life but "out of the heart." As with many romantics, maturity brought a slow wearing down of courage. His piano works and songs, written in his twenties and early thirties, are perhaps his most beautiful music, reflecting as they do the impetuous feelings stirred up by his courtship and love for Clara Schumann. They also sum up all his heroic proclamations of individuality against a society that seemed wholly antagonistic to him.

Both Berlioz and Schumann challenged the music criticism of their time, in which an entrenched political reaction took the form of dogmas about "correct style" and "taste." Both became brilliant music critics themselves. Schumann attacked the "philistines" and welcomed every fresh talent in the most self-effacing way. Among his "discoveries" were Chopin and Brahms. Berlioz wrote for the press to make a living, and also to defend himself. He said, "For the Press is, in a certain way, more precious than the spear of Achilles; not only does it occasionally heal the wounds which it has inflicted, but it also serves as a weapon of defense to the person who makes use of it."[6] Yet there is an unreality within the very feverish intensity of these critical tournaments, as if they did not carry on battles that were taking place in society itself, but rather transferred these feelings of oppression and protest to an ideal world of art. "Progress" came to be seen solely as a matter of destroying an old musical convention or welcoming a "daring" harmonic progression. Berlioz, the self-declared enemy of all conventions, who had in his youth been a partisan of the Revolution of 1830, looked upon the Revolution of 1848 with horror, crying, "Republicanism is at this moment passing like a vast roller over the face of the Continent. Musical art, which has been long dying, is now dead."[7] The new French Republic, as it happened, did recognize Berlioz' talents, but he did not blink at its subsequent overthrow, and willingly served the despotic Emperor Louis Napoleon. Schumann, who had reflected the revolutionary feelings of the 1830's with the stirring marches of the "Davidsbündler against the Philistines," as in his *Carnaval,* did write some "barricade marches" reflecting the events of 1849. But he was already suffering from the mental ailment that was to cause his death. Less flamboyant than Berlioz, his music expressed more deeply the yearning for love and for peaceful human relationships that makes romanticism appeal so deeply to the human heart.

6. Reaction in Life, "Progress" in Art

WHAT IS ACTUALLY MEANT by a "new music"? It can only mean a music which tackles new problems offered by society, thinks them through, and thus raises the art to a new level of realism. The composer who does this discovers at the same time that the heritage of musical form and technique he has taken over is inadequate. He must reshape it and carry it further. His new developments may be few compared to the heritage he uses, yet each is profound and electrifying, an advance in the power of music to reflect life.

This kind of progress is the opposite of what has passed for "new" and "modern" in the mainstream of bourgeois music from about 1830 on. Such music is more truly characterized as decadence. This does not mean that the music thus produced is lacking in beautiful and moving qualities. The works of Schumann, Berlioz, and Liszt, for example, are full of deep feeling and beauty. Decadence, however, means that the art as a whole, in its form and techniques, is brought down to a lower level of realism. Its power to reflect life in its fullness and to convey ideas is vitiated. The mentality behind it is thinner, for it is less social; it is the product of artistry which increasingly avoids the problems of life and struggle in the real world. At the same time this is accompanied by proclamations of the "revolutionary overthrow" of all previous musical forms and conventions. Such proclamations are themselves a sign of decadence, for there can be no real progress except by a full mastery of the best, most realistic achievements of the past. To wipe out the past, or pretend to, itself weakens the art. And it is true that the truly progressive masters of the past, such as Dufay, Bach, Mozart, Haydn, Beethoven, Schubert, never seemed to their times to be "moderns" in the sense the word has had from Liszt and Wagner on. They appeared, on the contrary, to be popularizers of music, even "vulgarizers" to some critics. While they had trouble with those who pretended to be arbiters of music, they had comparatively little trouble in being understood by their audiences. Now, however, the "modern" artist must appear to be "ahead" of his times, when the truth is that he falls behind them.

In the revolutionary movements of 1848, the working class emerged as an independent force, the most self-sacrificing in the struggle for republic and democracy, and also challenging the entire basis of the exploitation of labor by capital. The battles against monarchy and oligarchy, for constitutional government, seemed at first to be won in France, Germany, and Austria. But, as Engels writes, "the very victory of their class so shook the bourgeoisie of all countries that they fled back into the arms of the monarchist-feudal reaction which had just been overthrown."[1] In France, the workers who had led the victorious fighting for the republic were promised the suffrage, given jobs on public works, and disarmed. Then, when a pampered and anti-labor national guard could be organized, the workers were thrown out of their jobs, forced into revolt, and shot down. As a result the republic itself fell an easy prey to the adventurer, Louis Napoleon, who declared himself emperor in 1852. During 1848 and 1849 democratic uprisings gained control of Berlin and Vienna. But here too the weakness of the middle class, afraid to consolidate its own victories, caused the uprisings to be drowned in blood; and the promises of constitutions that had been made by terrified princes and their ministers were quickly withdrawn. Walt Whitman wrote of this period in his poem, "Europe —The 72nd and 73rd Years of These States":

The People scorned the ferocity of kings.
But the sweetness of mercy brew'd bitter destruction, and the
*   frighten'd monarchs come back,*
Each comes in state with his train, hangman, priest, tax-gatherer,
Soldier, lord, jailer, and sycophant. . . .

Meanwhile corpses lie in new-made graves, bloody corpses of
*   young men,*
The rope of the gibbet hangs heavily, the bullets of princes are
*   flying, the creatures of power laugh aloud. . . .*

Despite this destruction, Whitman saw hope for the future:

> *Not a grave of the murder'd for freedom but grows seed for*
> *freedom, in its turn to bear seed,*
> *Which the winds carry afar and re-sow, and the rains and the*
> *snows nourish. . . .*
> *Liberty, let others despair of you—I never despair of you."*

Characteristic of the main stream of bourgeois music, however, was that it abandoned its vague democratic yearnings of the 1830's and 1840's, and gave itself over to the service of reaction. What kind of musical progress can be created by such minds? As composers abandoned the real world of life and struggle, questions of musical style and form were furiously raised and debated. Should music be "pure," or should it have word, story, and "program"? Is the symphony a greater form than opera, or is it "old-fashioned"? Should folk song be used in musical composition or is it a "vulgarism"? Should music be tuneful, or should it abandon melody for harmonic progressions? Is chamber music the only true instrumental music, or should intelligent composers condescend to write for the concert hall? Such questions are unanswerable, for they are false to begin with. The achievements of such great masters as Bach, Mozart, Beethoven, and Schubert, working in every form, the simplest and the most complex, with words and without, each task assisting the other, made this process of setting one part of music against another obviously ridiculous. But the furious arguments, in which the public had nothing to say, indicate what happens when art is removed from real problems of social life, and when the crucial question of how art, in any form, can best reflect life and move people, is ignored. An escape from reality does not lead to peaceful life and art, but to more violent. Just as esthetics becomes torn by insoluble conflicts, so content becomes one of pessimism and violence, all the more harrowing because these storms now seem to come "from within."

Richard Wagner (1813-1883) had taken some part in the fighting in Dresden in 1849 and had to flee Germany. He quickly reconciled himself to living with the "powers that be," curried favor in France with the Emperor Louis Napoleon, became then a protégé of the young and half-insane king of Bavaria, and was pardoned by the German authorities. After 1870, when the needed step of the unification of Germany was taken under the rule of the most reactionary forces in German life—the Prussian Hohenzollerns and behind them the Krupp works, Wagner became the unofficial musical laureate of the new empire. His own life was typical of cutthroat bourgeois competitiveness at its most open and glaring. His hand was raised against every other man as a potential enemy. He curried favor from the French, then gloried in their defeat by the Germans. He took favors from leading Jewish musicians, and then assailed them in the vilest racist and anti-Semitic terms.

His art, which heavily borrowed even its melodies from Schubert songs, Schumann fantasies, Berlioz symphonies, and Liszt tone poems, thrust the music of his teachers into the background by offering itself as even more overwhelmingly "revolutionary," supplanting all previous musical forms. The new idea was to combine everything that had been previously done in music into the single form of opera. The music, he thundered, had to be a "means to an end," the end being the "drama." But to what was the drama a means? What was its relation to life? This was never answered. And in opera itself he moved away from the main reason for being of the form, the depiction of human beings and social relationships in terms of the human imagery of song. Everything was more gigantic, and more overwhelming in sense appeal, than anything seen and heard before. The operas were longer, the orchestras twice the size, the singing louder, the stage spectacles more glamorous. But all this battery of "new techniques" was designed to bludgeon the spectator out of asking, "What does all this mean?"

There is genius in Wagner. But the question that remains is the use to which it is put. The move from reality means inevitably that the art is reduced to a lower level. Wagner's vocal line is a reversion to primitive song-speech. It is not a retrogression to any actual art form of the past, but rather a primitive mentality and form speaking glibly of modern life and using all the "advanced" superficial techniques. Thus Wagner's song-speech, unlike that of primitive music, is dressed up with the richest musical naturalisms—depictions of wind, water, fire, thunderstorms, galloping horses, gods flying through the air—all of this requiring a phenomenal mastery of instrumental timbre and harmony. But naturalism drags thinking down to the level of the immediate sensation, abandoning all generalization, all real and clarifying thought. Similarly this highly elaborate song-speech, accenting each word with great finesse, abandons the task of genuinely representing in musical form the character doing the speaking. To this texture Wagner added the "leit-motifs," or a set of musical themes, associated with people or events on the stage. These constantly recur through the operas in shifting patterns, evoking memories in the mind of the listener of what has been seen before. The result, however, is nothing more than a "stream of consciousness," a masterful evocation of the *processes* of thought as a substitute for presenting the *content* of real thinking and the summation and results of thought.

Similarly the dramas themselves, except for the comedy, *The Mastersingers,* in which a recognizable society and credible human relationships appear, represent a kind of modern primitivism. It is not a return to the realities of primitive life, but a disguised use of primitive symbolism as the only tool in the artist's hands, and a most inadequate one, with which to deal with modern life. Primitive "magic" symbols and totems had been socially created as a force attempting to control what were then the still unmastered and mysterious forces of nature. Faced now by what are to him the mysterious forces of bourgeois life, the artist dredges up all these primitive symbolisms, no longer social but appearing to be psychological, representing the "inscrutable" forces at war in the mind. It is an abandonment of any attempt to discover the real forces creating these apparently mental disturbances. It is a product of the dissolution of conscious social relationships between the bourgeois individual and his fellow human being, so that every human desire meets unconquerable obstacles, human beings can never know one another, love is an uncontrollable obsession, and all events are the product of accident, mysterious curses, mystery, and "fate." The male heroes are dashing, stupid, infantile, as in the bourgeois dream of "freedom" and power, riding roughshod over all obstacles, surrounded by malicious enemies and triumphing over them, until defeated by an inexorable "destiny." The women are hailed as goddesses but are given no other function in life than to serve the male, so that when the "hero" dies they have no other recourse but to die also.

And the mythology drawn upon reflects precisely the ideology demanded by the German emperors and Krupps, disguising their real military operations in mystic terms of a German "racial" destiny and hypocritical religious clothing. It is made up of German tribal sagas and rituals, of medieval German tales of chivalry mixing feudal arrogance with infantile magic. It is no accident that the Nazi psychoanalyst, Carl Jung, drew heavily upon Wagner for his theories of inherited myths and the "racial unconscious" as the dominating force in the human mind. Even *The Mastersingers,* which has a semblance of realism in its portrayal of sixteenth century German society, ignores the great peasant revolts and proclaims a mystic German unity of the knight and the burgher, while the lesser common people look on in adoration.

Wagner himself has become a figure of bourgeois myth. For the bourgeois world to have analyzed him realistically would have demanded that bourgeois life itself be analyzed critically. More books have been written about him than about any other composer, generally accepting him on his own evaluation as a maligned genius, the summation of all previous music, and the master of "meanings" which cannot be clearly defined because they are too "deep." The very mountain of interpretive literature that has been piled up is a sign of reversion to the archaic concept of art not as a reflection of the real world but as a ritual, a collection of oracles, or "sacred book," requiring the mystic and constantly differing interpretations of a priesthood. In fact, not only at the "shrine" Wagner built at Bayreuth but also in the Metropolitan Opera House in New York, Wagner's works are presented not as ordinary operas but almost as a religious ritual. The fact that so much subsequent music seemed to follow the paths he laid down is offered as proof of his "revolutionary" and prophetic character. Yet this "influence" means only that as the crises, contradictions, havoc, and war of monopoly capital multiply, the middle class, spinelessly leaving the control of the real world to the hands of the most reactionary forces, finds an increasingly attractive refuge in Wagner's heroic gestures in the land of dreams. He did foreshadow many of the cultural currents that have become the mainstream of unrealism today. The second act of *Tristan and Isolde,* for example, is a "night piece," in which the "day," when real life and actions are carried on, is proclaimed to be full of "falsehoods" and "phantoms." Only night and its dreams are real. His last opera, *Parsifal,* foreshadows the religious revival among present-day "intellectuals," like T. S. Eliot, Stravinsky, Schönberg, and Dali. In *Parsifal,* there is no flicker of the deep human feelings found in past religious art, when real social struggles in the real world were sometimes carried on in religious terms. Nor is there any real conviction. In *Parsifal* as today, primitive myth and magic, Catholicism, Protestantism, belief in witchcraft, cabbalism, Buddhism, philosophic pessimism, "sex temptations," are all rolled together.

Johannes Brahms (1833-1897), twenty years younger, was born in Hamburg, lived most of his life in or near Vienna, and came to maturity wholly in the reactionary atmosphere that followed 1848. He had nothing like Wagner's youthful revolutionary experiences and, unlike Wagner, felt no need to offer propaganda for reaction in the name of "revolutionary art." Where Wagner offered all his works as flamboyant sense appeal and elaborate pageant, Brahms shuddered away from contact with public life. Although he wrote four symphonies and four concertos, all at the cost of great travail, the form he favored most was chamber music, which he made a medium for his most personal, introspective, yearning, and pessimistic reflections. Where Wagner proclaimed that he was overthrowing all previous musical conventions, Brahms proclaimed a feeling of relative impotence, and wrote as if he could only follow humbly in the footsteps of such great men of the past as Bach, Haydn, Mozart, Beethoven, and Schubert, although the truth is that the harmonic complications of the "modern" school can be traced back as much to Brahms as to Wagner.

Brahms did not offer his music as a world view of triumphant reaction, but took the attitude of a medieval craftsman who left politics and all such matters to the lords of the manor. He childishly gloried in the victories of the German armies over Austria, Denmark, and France. Ironically, his will, which left the bulk of his fortune to a society for the aid of struggling young musicians, was broken after his death with the connivance of the Prussian government he so admired. Such a bequest was apparently "too socialistic." He created works of music with the careful, sound workmanship of an honest master guildsman of the Middle Ages, enriched as in the case of Wagner with all the techniques and methods that had been learned from Beethoven and the great achievements of realism. His meanings are cloudy in a different way from Wagner's. The music is offered not as mystical symbol but as "pure feeling," and of course the feelings, so wordlessly offered, relate to nothing but the real world of his time. Although as a citizen Brahms followed the path of the junkers and empire builders, as a musician he says that this is a world of melancholy disappointment. His great insight is that he realizes the need to preserve at least in form the most heroic qualities of past music. He not only extracts the lessons he needs from the great music of the past, but partly rewrites and reworks that music. It is not done in an imitative or plagiaristic spirit. Rather, just as Brahms feels that the world is somehow running down, so his emotions are bound up with the great works of the heroic past, which are more real to him than the life about him. And so it is from these works that he draws, as more realistic composers draw experience from life. All human relationships appear difficult and complicated, and so in his music the expression of the simplest feeling becomes complicated and full of reservations. Everything is said through indirection; joy melts into sadness, and powerful outbursts of protest dissolve into resignation. There is a deep reaching out to the "folk," seen in his songs and the many folk-dance finales of his chamber works, but the "folk" are also seen in medieval terms, as "simple" people whose joys come because they are so carefree.

The wordy battle between the followers of Wagner and of Brahms did not represent the partisanship which examines art to find what is outmoded, and what must be done to suit the needs of real people in a changing world. Rather, it represented only the one-sidedness that bourgeois culture increasingly takes, with each offshoot demanding that it be accepted as the one "true art." Wagner's "advances" were offered as a critique and answer to Brahms's looking toward the past, his worship of the old masters, his acceptance of a relatively impotent role in social life. Brahms's music is a critique and exposure of the essential windiness, silliness, and unreality of Wagner's "revolution," its battles in the clouds. Each was right about the other. Wagner leads directly to such contemporary composers as Schönberg, whose works are full of harrowing cries, dream symbols, and proclamations of the mysterious power of the "unconscious." Brahms leads directly to such contemporary composers as Hindemith, a musician to his fingertips, who turns out finely contrived contrapuntal works in the spirit of the German craftsmen-composers of the seventeenth century, and whose more emotionally expressive works are only elegies and requiems.

Brahms reminds one of the late Beethoven, who also lived in a period of reaction. But where Beethoven's anguish and protest end in a feeling of victorious faith in humanity, Brahms' protest ends in a feeling of tragic resignation to a life too much for him to cope with. Certainly nobody has expressed this tragic resignation better than Brahms does, in his late chamber and piano works.

The power in Wagner and Brahms which tends to disarm criticism is that they are such great craftsmen. Although their range of human portrayal is so narrow, their meanings are so meager, their world view so backward, they still seem to write so well. Everything is in the best possible musical taste. Yet this power itself is a product of the great musical revolution and realistic techniques that had been created during the century before them. And this "old master" polish of their music comes from the fact that in the period of bourgeois decline, they remained wholly within the bourgeois world view. They added no really new human images to previous music, but only refinements, complications, and subjective probings. To have wrestled with the political developments of their day, to have awakened to the great popular movements and sought to express them in music, would have meant awakening to new musical problems that could not be so easily and "tastefully" handled. It might even have meant the entrance of elements in their music that scholars would refer to as "crude" and "vulgar." Such "crudities" and "vulgarities," as snobbish critics considered them, were found in abundance in Verdi's operas, which were a partisan weapon of the Italian struggle for national liberation, and in the works of the great Russian national composers. Yet it was these latter works that really brought new human imagery, meaning, and content to the music of the later nineteenth century, and which carried on the triumphs of musical realism with which the century had opened.

7. Music and National Freedom

NATIONAL MUSIC DOES NOT consist of a language, a system of putting tones together, unique to one nation and incomprehensible to others. It consists basically of musical works, of folk songs, dances, and large-scale compositions, created by the people in their struggles for progress, and by composers with close ties to the people, which have become part of the living cultural history and artistic treasure house of each nation. These national works can be deeply moving to people of other nations.

National cultures rose along with the development of nations under capitalism. This development of national cultures was also accompanied by the suppression of national cultures, as one nation asserted its economic, political, and cultural domination over others. Within the culture of bourgeois nations, many cultures of minority peoples were suppressed or kept from growing. Just as national struggles have been a continuous part of history from the sixteenth century up to the present, as one nation after another fought for independence or struggled out of feudal backwardness, so the rise of national cultures has been a continuous process in music history from the sixteenth century to the present. A national music, like a nation, goes through constant change and development. Its materials may in part be a tribal heritage of ritual music and songs of ancient bards. Its folk music stems from tribal music but also takes whatever it finds useful from other musical cultures. Its composed works of music, which reflect the struggles for nationhood, use folk music and in turn influence folk music. Thus the Lutheran chorales composed in Germany, the Elizabethan songs and madrigals and the melodies of Handel in England, the songs of Haydn and Schubert in Austria, the songs written by Chopin for the Polish people, have become more than the personal expressions of their composers. They belong to the nation. The composer may be called

73

an intermediary, who returns in enriched form the material he has gotten from the people, reflecting in the process the conditions of life of the nation in his own time. By so doing, he is only repeating on a far higher level of formal development the process of creation of folk art itself, for folk art was the product of innumerable anonymous individuals of talent, each contributing something new to the common cultural possessions. In the period of anti-feudal struggle, whatever is progressive and lasting in the arts inevitably takes a national form, for its rise accompanies the rise of the nations themselves. Yet the tendency of an advanced capitalist country is to deny the national character of the arts, for the rise to nationhood of other peoples, and the national aspirations of peoples within its own borders, are a menace to its own ruling class.

Grand opera, born in Italy, had lost most of its national character with the decline of the Italian city-states, and had become a formalized, cosmopolitan entertainment for the feudal courts of Europe. With the rising struggles for Italian unity and independence, touched off by Napoleon's campaigns in Italy in 1796, opera began to take on a national character again in the work of such composers as Gioachino Antonio Rossini (1792-1868), Gaetano Donizetti (1797-1848), and Vincenzo Bellini (1801-1835). This character appeared partly in the guise of comedies of village life, partly in historical melodramas based on stories from Sir Walter Scott and Schiller which had anti-feudal implications. All of these works drew upon folk and popular song to create an appealing lyrical human imagery. The giant who raised opera to a new level of realism, carrying it a long way toward the faithful depiction of history and society, and toward the rounded-out musical portrayal of human beings, was the peasant-born Giuseppe Verdi (1813-1901). He was able to do this because he made opera a conscious weapon of the Italian democratic and national struggles.

Verdi had to combat the censorship, direct and indirect, of the Austrian police and the Roman Catholic Church. An edict of Pope Leo XII, governing behavior in the theaters of Rome during the 1840's, prohibited an actor from interpolating a word or gesture not found in the prompt-book, on pain of being sent to the galleys for five years. Applause and hisses could be rewarded by a prison term of two months to a half year. Verdi's political allusions had to be made in symbolic form, but with symbols, unlike Wagner's primitive myth and magic, provided by real history and with realistic social meaning. In his early opera, *Nabucco,* for example, dealing with the Biblical Jews enslaved by Nebuchadnezzar, the cries to revolt against oppression had obvious significance to Italian audiences. Verdi set the chorus of the Jews yearning for their homeland to a broad, swinging melody in popular style, which immediately became the rage throughout Italy. There were similar parallels in his music dramas of the struggle of the Lombard League in the twelfth century against the invading German emperor, and in the outcries against tyranny of his outlaw-heroes such as Manrico in *Il Trovatore* and Ernani. Many of his operas, which are snobbishly regarded today as blood-and-thunder melodrama, were among the first to show the feudal nobility in their true oppressive nature, with their bloody feuds and insensate concepts of family "honor" masking the most arrogant egotism. He gave the common people, such as the gipsy mother in *Il Trovatore* and the townspeople in *Falstaff,* the most warm and affecting musical characterizations. He broadened the entire human scope of opera with profound musical portrayals of characters like Violetta in *La Traviata* and Rigoletto, seeing a far deeper humanity in these victims of the nobility than in the nobility themselves.

The great weapon in his arsenal of realism was song. This he could create prolifically and bend to a variety of uses, making it express the most open feelings and the most sensitive portrayals of mood and conflict. Song alone does not create realism, but the presence of song affirms the presence of living human beings as the material of the drama, and without this there can be no realism. The great song writer, in the words of the Russian Glinka, "arranges the music of the people." Verdi brought to opera a wealth of Italian folk melody, creating as well new melodies that became beloved by the people and sung in the streets. Thus his art had two lives, one on the stage and the other on people's lips. This turn of music to the service of the people was in no way a "vulgarization" or "simplification" except in the worthwhile sense that everything in the operas was designed to be understood.

Verdi did not take the step of representing the history of his own time in music, and his portrayal of past history had limitations. Frequently the struggles for freedom were portrayed as if they had been carried on solely by noble personages, and the cliché persisted of presenting social struggles in terms of love affairs cutting across the opposing camps, in *Romeo and Juliet* manner.

Verdi's deep but incomplete realism is typical of many of the great bourgeois realists, who are baffled by the manner in which corrupt politics denies what the people had fought for and the needs of the people themselves. Thus they proclaim themselves aloof from solution. Verdi, elected to the Italian legislative assembly, wrote in 1870, "I cannot reconcile the idea of Parliament with the College of Cardinals, a free press with the Inquisition, civil law with the Syllabus. I am frightened at the way our government goes ahead any old way, hoping that time will take care of everything."[1] He wrote again in 1881, "For you know, you inhabitants of the city, that the misery among the poor is great, very great, much too great—and if nothing is done about it, either from above or below, some time or other a catastrophe will result. . . . Look! If I were the government, I wouldn't bother so much about the parties, about the Whites, the Reds, or the Blacks. I'd bother about the daily bread that the people must have to eat. But don't let's talk about politics—I know nothing about politics, and I can't stand them, at least not the kind we have had up to now."[2] His *Othello*, written in 1888 and based on Shakespeare's play, may be said to reflect the situation in Italy itself, with its opening cries of "Victory" and its inspired portrayal of the tragic soldier and hero destroyed by the machinations of Iago, the self-seeking politician.

Russian national music differed from the almost single-handed efforts of Verdi in Italy in that it was a collective creation of a number of men of genius, each stimulating the other. Starting with Michael Glinka (1804-1857) and Alexander Dargomijsky (1813-1869), who devoted themselves largely to opera, it flowered in the work of the "Five": Modest Mussorgsky (1835-1881), Mily Balakirev (1837-1910), Alexander Borodin (1834-1887), Cesar Cui (1835-1918), and Nikolai Rimsky-Korsakov (1844-1908). The "Five" taught each other, studied, criticized, and fought for each other's work, with a self-effacing devotion to the creation of a truly national music, representing the nation's history and the greatness and character of its people. Opera remained the core of their work, but they also moved into song, tone poem, symphony, and piano music. Another great figure who stood somewhat apart from them was Peter Ilyich Tchaikovsky (1840-1893).

This musical creativity was an integral part of a sweeping national cultural movement which included literature and the graphic arts, and produced a body of novels, poetry, satire, and criticism second to none in the century. The writing was outstanding for its partisanship on behalf of the oppressed people, its popular character even when it seemed as if it could not reach the greatest part of the masses in its own time, its devotion to the battle of ideas and search for truth, its opposition to every form of hypocrisy and fraud no matter how deeply entrenched in government. And this democratic cultural movement in turn reflected a century of developing social struggle in the nation itself, starting with the guerrilla movements of the peasantry against Napoleon in 1812, and the struggles against serfdom, continuing with the revolt of the "Decembrists," a liberal group of the nobility, in 1825, reaching a new level with the freeing of the serfs in 1861, going on to peasant uprisings, the organization and militant struggles of the working class, culminating in the Revolution of 1905. These social struggles at first found their most articulate voice in cultural works. Their leadership at first came from a left-wing minority among the nobility. Then in the 1840's middle class figures rose to leadership, and, at the end of the century, great working class figures.

A host of great musical works were set to the dramas, poems, stories, and folklore collections of Alexander Pushkin (1799-1837), the great poet of African ancestry who was a friend of the "Decembrists." A guiding spirit of the "Five" was Vladimir Stasov (1820-1890), a folklorist, art and music critic, who was a friend and admirer of the powerful anti-tsarist, democratic, and socialist polemicists, Belinsky, Nikolai Dobroliubov (1836-1861), and Nikolai Chernishevsky (1828-1889). Tchaikovsky, who regarded himself as a conservative in politics, was deeply influenced by Leo Tolstoy, who wrote such sentiments as "Science and art have forwarded the progress of mankind. Yes; but this was not done by the fact that men of science and art, under the pretext of a division of labor, taught men by word, and chiefly by deed, to utilize by violence the misery and sufferings of the people, in order to free themselves from the very first and unquestionable human duty of laboring with their hands in the common struggle of mankind with nature."[3] Tchaikovsky made it a goal of his own art "to reach out to the hearts of as many people as possible."

It was necessary for Russian composers to take this progressive path. If they had a genuine interest in creating truly Russian music, they had to turn to the people for their material. In doing this, they had to discover the true life, the miseries and struggles of the people. In building an art on this base, even in rediscovering past history and fostering a national consciousness, they found themselves in direct opposition to tsarism and the decadent aristocracy, who welcomed the exploitation of the land, its people and resources by British and French capital and fought with ruthless violence every move to better the lot of the peasantry and working class. Thus Russian national music rose in a constant battle against cosmopolitanism, which showed itself in the importation of the lightest Italian opera and the admiration for everything "French" in the courts and salons. When Glinka's opera, *Ivan Susanin,* was first performed, with its peasant hero and use of Russian folk idiom, titled listeners complained that it was "coachmen's music." Cosmopolitanism also took the form of a "German academicism" taught in the music schools, according to which musical composition was a matter of knowing the "correct rules of harmony" presumably ordained from on high. The rejection of cosmopolitanism, however, did not mean insularity and provincialism. Just as the great Russian social critics and philosophers had been inspired by the French Encyclopedists such as Diderot, so the national composers studied Beethoven's music and everything that they thought was ground-breaking in the realm of human expression from the work of Schumann, Berlioz, and Liszt.

The operas of the Russian national school are in general distinguished by a high literary quality of text, a naturalness in the presentation of human characters in music and action, and a faithfulness to history of a kind previously unknown in opera. Human love is dealt with, but it no longer decides the fate of nations and empires. Works like Borodin's *Prince Igor,* Mussorgsky's *Boris Godunov* and *Khovantchina* present history realistically, and in *Boris* the people themselves are a powerful protagonist of the drama. Even in fairy tale, the emphasis is on the folk and social meanings of the old stories, and Rimsky-Korsakov's *The Golden Cockerel* was censored because its fantasy telling of a stupid king going off to war was considered a reflection on the tsar's war with Japan in 1904-05. There is an absence of vocal display for its own sake. In works like the above, and in Tchaikovsky's operas such as *Eugene Onegin* and *Queen of Spades,* the melodic line and construction of the vocal passages follow the intonations and rhythms of speech, and yet the music is not declamation. Character is always expressed through genuinely lyrical and songful invention.

The operas, along with the tone poems, songs, symphonic works, and chamber music, exhibit the riches to be found in folk music, and the free, varied, and expressive uses to which these riches may be put. In the songs and operas of Mussorgsky the words "folk" or "folk style" embrace a multitude of different musical forms and human images, used for peasant characters and kings, sometimes a free semi-speech and semi-song music and sometimes a square-cut strophic song, sometimes sounding major or minor, sometimes modal, sometimes Asian in origin. And in Mussorgsky "folk style" sounds wholly different from the way it sounds in Glinka, Borodin, Rimsky-Korsakov, and Tchaikovsky. Nor does "folk" ever mean childish simplicity, or primitivism. Characters such as Boris Godunov, or Tchaikovsky's Tatiana and Onegin in *Eugene Onegin,* are profound psychological portrayals in music as well as word. They are mature, fully conscious, and grown-up people. There are not many operatic characters who share this quality. One thinks of Mozart's Figaro and Susanna, Verdi's Othello, Desdemona, Lady Macbeth, and Simon Boccanegra, Wagner's Hans Sachs. With Wagner's Tristan, Isolde, Siegfried, and Brunnhilde, and with most of the characters of "modern" opera, such as Strauss's *Salome* and *Elektra,* Debussy's *Pelléas and Mélisande,* Berg's *Wozzeck,* we are back with the child mind, the obsessed, and the "unconscious."

Tchaikovsky found himself in opposition to the "Five." The differences were not deep, however, and rose out of the narrowness of music patronage of the time. Progress could not be debated solely in terms of the real needs of people and the changes demanded of music, but had to take the form of one camp as against another, each backed by different patrons and journalists. What alienated Tchaikovsky from the "Five" was what he felt to be their one-sidedness and even amateurishness. In the necessary rejection of academicism, the "Five" found themselves with few tools left. Adding to this the fact that they had to support themselves through means other than music, they worked with painful slowness, leaving many works unfinished. Yet the "Five" saw the main task of Russian music in their time, which was to affirm the relation of music to life by associating it with real images of people, history, and drama. Only on such a base could a more generalized and "philosophical" music of symphony and chamber music be built, and remain meaningful to the people. Tchaikovsky took the next step, which was to build a musical culture that could satisfy a variety of people's needs and express every side of life. Thus he set himself the task of building Russian music on a more scholarly basis, encouraging conservatory study and exploring symphony, tone poem, sonata, and chamber music, along with opera and song.

Tchaikovsky's music is sometimes described as "morbid" or expressive of the "Slavic soul," the stereotype used to hide the profoundly social character of progressive nineteenth century Russian art. Taken as a whole, including the symphonies, concertos, ballets, operas, songs, and chamber music, his work is a many-sided music with much joy in life. He suffered from harrowing personal problems, and his works, such as *Queen of Spades* and the "Pathétique" Symphony, often express a deep anguish. But it is never pessimistic or morbid, for it never resigns itself to the rejection of life. There is always the struggle for life. His symphonies reaffirm the nature of the form as it had been developed in the hands of Beethoven, a public message on an epic level, intended to be clear and understood in every bar. There is never any question as to what any passage in the music means, or a passage inserted by the demands of symmetry or formal rules. The listener feels a close kinship with the human being thus speaking to him through melody and harmony. The same clarity of statement is found in his chamber music. For a generation after Tchaikovsky's death critics wrote snobbishly about his music, as if its very popularity with audiences made it suspect. This only meant, however, that the masses with whom this music was popular were ahead of the critics. They recognized a composer who respected them as human beings, felt kin to them, and even, in the best sense of the word, obligated to those whose labor made his own work possible.

8. *How Modern Is Modern?*

THE MOST STRIKING CHARACTERISTIC of the "advanced" music produced under capitalism in the twentieth century is that it is uncomprehended and unloved. This fact is sometimes explained on the theory that it is the work of the misunderstood "genius" of our time, which represents the "future," and must naturally be baffling to all but a few today. Yet it cannot be said that these "advanced" modern composers are unknown, friendless, unrecognized, starving in garrets. Some, like the late Arnold Schönberg (1874-1951), were attacked by critics in their youth. Today, however, Schönberg, Igor Stravinsky (1882—), and Paul Hindemith (1895—) are most highly respected and publicized figures. In the United States they hold leading teaching positions, and their theories of music have become the dominant ones taught in the music schools. Their followers are music critics for the leading newspapers and write prolifically for the scholarly journals. Their work is performed, published, and available for study on phonograph recordings. Books are written expounding their theories, and in fact they are the most "explained" composers in history. The veil, thrown about this music, that it is a "rebellion" against the modern world, was always a thin one, and now it is threadbare. The music and the theories are accepted today in what were traditionally the centers of the staunchest conservatism and reaction, the press and the academies. The only "rebellion" seems to be that among the great mass of music lovers, who find that they are able to like few or none of these works.

No art can be "of the future." It describes its own age, in clear or confused terms. If it embraces those ideas which in its own time reflect what is being born, rising, and most alive, as against what is dying, then it may break ground for the future. But such art, precisely because its roots are in the real experiences and problems that most people share, is the most comprehensible. The reason for the unlovable and seemingly incomprehensible character of twentieth century "advanced" music is that, going a stage beyond the nineteenth century "modernism" of Liszt and Wagner, or Brahms's pull to the classic past, it becomes militantly anti-realistic. It denies even the possibility of human imagery, ideas, and meaning in music.

It is the art of an age of imperialism, an art which does not look upon imperialism critically, but typifies the total mystification of economic, social, and historical forces which imperialism spreads in people's minds. Imperialism is an economy dominated by giant monopolies, trusts, banking chains, and cartels. It is a stage of constant struggle for redivision of world trade, markets, and raw materials, and of constant war tension and war. Faced by growing struggles for national independence in colonial nations, and by the organization of labor at home, imperialism begins to circumscribe, negate, and in the final extreme abandon the parliamentary democracy and the human and civil rights brought into being in the struggles of capitalism against feudalism. It produces fascism.

It is this development of capitalism itself which explains the seeming "rebellion" of twentieth century "advanced" music. This music is no rebellion against the ruling economic and political powers. Rather, the real world must be shrouded in mystery and declared "unreal." The rebellion is against realism itself, and more specifically against the great humanist tradition of realistic drama, ideas, love of people, and joy in life, that was born in the struggle of the bourgeoisie against feudalism. This "revolt" showed itself in two general ways. In the realm of "pure" or "absolute" music, the great concert-hall symphonic forms were abandoned. The epic and heroic symphony was considered "nineteenth century." The "advanced" composers either touched this form not at all, or occasionally wrote travesties, satires on the symphony, "miniature" symphonies, exercises in the symphony form as if it were simply one among many little bundles of rules and formalities. Replacing the symphony and purporting to be an "advance" fit for the "twentieth century" appeared nothing more than little serenades, "divertimentos," collections of eighteenth century aristocratic dances, medieval liturgical pieces, and exercises in counterpoint. This movement back to the Middle Ages or to the forms of aristocratic music of the seventeenth and eighteenth centuries was known as "neo-classicism." In the realm of music with story or stage action, such as opera, ballet, and tone poem, the "revolt" showed itself in an imagery which resembled no real people and human relationships that exist now or ever existed in history. Instead, ancient myths or blood-curdling stories were presented in which the characters were offered as symbols and representations of tensions and drives in the unconscious mind. The outstanding twentieth century "advanced" operas, for example, are Richard Strauss's *Elektra* (1909), Claude Debussy's *Pelléas and Mélisande* (1902), and Alban Berg's *Wozzeck* (1921). *Elektra* purports to use the old Greek legend used by Aeschylus, Sophocles, and Euripides, but compared to the "modern" version, those of the ancient Greeks are masterpieces of rational thought and human portrayal. The Strauss opera has no relation to life or to Greek culture but is really a medieval "Dance of Death." The word "blood" occurs about twenty times in the text, and typical of the horrible lines are "And may the blood from severed throats fall upon thy tomb! And like urns upturned, may it flow. . . ." Typical stage directions are "screaming like a wounded animal," or "Silently like a wild animal, she creeps along the wall of the house." The characters are depicted as killing each other and driven like the obsessed, bound in unconscious mother-son, sister-brother, father-daughter erotic attachments of a "modern" Freudian derivation. *Pelléas and Mélisande* is a fairy tale full of pathos and mystery, in which the characters are impotent and oppressed as in a nightmare or hallucination. *Wozzeck* is a bloody murder story, in which the common people are portrayed both as victims of malicious cruelty, and as pathetic idiots.

In the early years of the century, the "radical" composers still carried the romantic air of being lonely art-heroes combating the bourgeois philistines. In this character Strauss wrote his autobiographical tone poem, calling it *A Hero's Life,* and Schönberg, in 1913, when one of his works was finally applauded, refused to acknowledge the applause, saying, "For years the people who cheered me tonight refused to recognize me. Why should I thank them for appreciating me now?"[1] It is also true that the more academic and conservative minds in these years were puzzled, shocked, and offended by this depiction of horrors, the obvious revelation of decadence and proclamation of irrationality as a way of thought, the turn to the archaic in the name of "advance." When the first World War exhibited the horrors of which the "civilized" world of monopoly capital was capable, including a lively trade in materials of war among the warring countries, formalist and irrational subjectivism became dominant trends in bourgeois musical life. They intensified their air of rebellion, describing themselves as the product of "disillusion." It was truly a period of revolution, which saw the overthrow of the Russian tsarist autocracy and the emergence of the socialist Soviet Union. The character of these "advanced" musical trends, however, was the opposite of what had happened in Russia. In the Soviet Union Lenin was proclaiming, "Unless we clearly understand that only by acquiring exact knowledge of the culture created by the whole development of mankind and that only by re-working this culture, can a proletarian culture be built, we shall not be able to solve this problem. . . . Proletarian culture must be the result of a natural development of the stores of knowledge which mankind has accumulated under the yoke of capitalist society, landlord society and bureaucratic society."[2] The "advanced" bourgeois trends, however, with their talk of a "revolution" of "musical tones," "new languages" the overturn of "tradition," had the effect of leaving the real world in the hands of the masters of capital, while art lost all connection with human imagery.

Thus it is not surprising that after the second World War, which saw the destruction of the fascist armies, the turning of new countries to socialism, and the appearance of the People's Republic of China, these anti-realist trends became even more dominant and dictatorial in the imperialist world. They flourished wherever there were great concentrations of monopoly, virulent hatred of socialism, support of the remnants of fascism, theories of the inevitability of war. They became agents of ignorance and weapons of reaction. If mankind could not be convinced that the capitalist world was pleasant, humane, and progressive, it could at least be told that the world was irrational, mad, and chaotic, run by the mystic laws of "human nature" and the "unconscious," and that people were therefore powerless to change it.

The incomprehensibility of the musical works produced out of such trends is a product not of any depth of thought or true difficulties they represent, but of the appended theoretical explanations and proclamations about the "world of the future," the "machine age symphonies," the "liberation of the unconscious," which have no relation whatsoever to the music. The music is easy to appraise, once the listener realizes that he is faced with a deliberately unreal subject, a mental process devoted to the irrational, the dream, and the nightmare, and a musical form and material drawn from the archaic. This kind of music was divided into two main trends. One, the "atonal," was centered in Vienna mainly about the work of Arnold Schönberg. The other, the "polytonal," was centered in Paris. Its leading figure was Igor Stravinsky, who was born in Russia but whose early ballets had been written for Paris. A landowner who refused to return to Russia after 1919, he spent the 1920's and 1930's in Paris and today lives in the United States.

The atonal school offered itself as the new, twentieth century step in the musical tradition opened up by the great Viennese classical composers, Haydn, Mozart, Beethoven, Schubert. In truth, it did represent one thin thread of this tradition, for it arose from the mentality of the petty-bourgeoisie who had once been part of the revolutionary movement against feudalism. But today the petty-bourgeoisie finds its "freedom," the "freedom" of the market place, has turned into oppressive and mysterious chains. Something of this middle class decline had been reflected in the philosophic pessimism of Wagner and Brahms. Now it turns to a lurid dabbling with images of anarchistic violence and horror, as if the very fears of the real world which it rejects and refuses to recognize come back with redoubled force and appear as the outcries of the "unconscious." It is called atonal because it carries forward the subjective uses of harmony, the movement from key to key and the use of chromatic tones, or half-steps outside the keys, to the point where all sense of key or of a tonal resting place is lost. There are no longer "consonances" and "dissonances" but only various degrees of dissonance, with the result that the music is in a constant state of tension which ends by defeating its own purpose, leaving the listener unmoved. Because it rejects experiences and human images from the real world, its experiences become those of past music. It is saturated with memories of the music of Haydn and Mozart, Beethoven and Schubert, Wagner and Brahms, from which it draws only the most extreme moments, like Don Giovanni's last shuddering cry, the occasional wide leaps of the voice in a Schubert song, or a dissonant chord, a portentous silence, an introspective passage of inde-terminate tonality from a Beethoven sonata. Atonality reached an emotional peak in the work of Alban Berg (1885-1935), which por-trayed the genuine horror and impotence of the middle class after the first World War and in the face of the rise of fascism. It reached a dead end in the work of Anton Webern (1883-1945), in which the labor of years produces a piece of music lasting a few minutes and, despite the formal complications in the work, the listener hears only tensions between one isolated note or chord and the next, and twangs followed by silences.

"Polytonality," on the other hand, militantly rejects the classical and nineteenth century romantic heritage. It declares that it is opposed to the expression of psychological states in music. It offers music as an exercise in pure form, and presents the musician as an artisan, or sometimes as a "scientist" of acoustics and the handling of instrumen-tal timbres. Actually it is a rejection of the scientific world view, of the knowledge of history, and of social life. It is a flight back to the musical cultures of feudal, slave, and primitive societies. These past cultures are not viewed, or re-created as they really were, but are imagined as a kind of dream world that never existed, in which there was "peace," "innocence," no movement of time, no sense of change.

The strangeness of sound in most polytonal music, referred to as "freshness" by its admirers, is actually the re-emergence of ancient primitive, folk, medieval, and Asian scales, and percussive rhythms independent of melody, replacing the major-minor scales and the principles of harmonic movement that were based on them. The music shows no real understanding of these non-European musical cultures, nor does it attempt to use and build upon the human imagery in them. On the contrary, this movement is an intellectual pose of flight from "civilization" to a fancied "primitive," a search for strange and exotic sounds. It actually reflects the imperialist attitude toward oppressed colonial peoples as "backward" and "primitive" while it patronizingly admires their "strange and colorful" ways of life. In actuality, it is the composer who becomes backward, disguising his own poverty-stricken humanity in a costume taken from other cultures. In the music, the combination of instrumental timbres becomes a dominating force, controlling the harmony, and this is a retrogression rather than an advance. Form becomes not a product of the understanding of the movement and pattern of life, but only of the mastery of tools, manipulated as if the only thing real to the artist were what he could actually feel and touch. In most of Stravinsky's music, construction becomes a simple matter of "ostinatos," little phrases or rhythmic figures repeated over and over again, while other rhythmic figures or lines of "endless melody," as in primitive music, but without its human feeling, are piled up in layers upon layers. In most formalistic music, for all the talk about form, the form itself is ridiculously simple, even infantile. It cannot be otherwise, because the reflection of life is absent or infantile. What gives this music the appearance of great accomplishment and complexity is the fact that its archaic patterns mix together many different modes and scales of the ancient past, clothed in the full panoply of modern orchestral dress.

Polytonal music went through many metamorphoses, each one showing it to be more poverty-stricken. In Debussy's "impressionism," for all its sensitivity and sweetness of melody, the music tended toward a kind of mindlessness, as if the composer were thinking of himself as a cloud, a goldfish, the waves moved by the winds, living in purely passive and visceral sensations, while Asian and old French folk scales showed themselves as a kind of exotic color. Stravinsky's ballets before the first World War, such as the *Rites of Spring,* used old Russian folk phrases of melody, in mechanistic rhythmic patterns, as if the composer were describing the folk as "simple minds" or automatons. An admirer thus describes one of the works of this period, *The Wedding*: "If the music seems jerky and the phrases short, the listener must be reminded of the immature minds predominant in an atmosphere of primitive culture."[3] The truth is that the common people at that time were about to carry through one of the great social changes of history, and Stravinsky's concept of the "simple folk" must be classed as wishful thinking. As for the "jerky" phrases and "immature" atmosphere, they are rather dear to Stravinsky because they are used again in his works dedicated to praise of Apollo and the church.

During the 1920's a number of composers of polytonal music appeared in France, such as Darius Milhaud, Arthur Honegger, and François Poulenc. There was sometimes a pleasant satiric quality about their music, which exploited many kinds of exotic and fancied "primitive" melody and rhythm, and even used fragments of jazz and music-hall tunes. Yet at best this music was devastatingly thin, disguising this thinness of content with a shock quality of ingenious instrumental sounds and dissonances. It was sometimes described as a return to "classicism," and it may be in a sense the twentieth century Parisian ghost of the "neo-classicism" of the French Second Empire, which had itself been a revival of the mock "classicism" of Louis XIV, which in turn had been a mock revival of the classic art of ancient Greece. It was when Stravinsky settled in Paris that he adopted "neo-classicism," using the same thin constructions as in his previous work but now imitating the rhythms of eighteenth century French dances instead of the "primitive," and filling his music with fragments of melody borrowed from a host of past composers.*

The latest stage for Stravinsky, largely worked out in the United States, is a "religious revival"—a bare chanting with almost purely visceral effect on the listener and denuded of human imagery. He has also turned to quoting his past works. At the same time his music is protected from any real critical examination by a number of his disciple-composers, who also write prolific "criticism" in which all Stravinsky's faults are transmuted into virtues. Thus to one such American disciple and publicist, Arthur Berger, Stravinsky's very poverty-stricken feeding on his own past becomes a "searching spirit." "Stravinsky's latest tendency to consolidate all his findings and restate them in new terms is but one more evidence of his constantly searching spirit. . . . Now his music reflects almost the entire range of his earlier styles. Such inclusiveness would have been unthinkable before." When Stravinsky shows himself unable to communicate recognizable human emotion, Berger writes, "His almost perverse avoidance of the obvious sentiments of tragedy is communicated with masterly cunning."[4]

For all the sometimes bitter argument that went on for some decades between the subjectivist and formalist schools, the paper-thin barrier between the two eventually collapsed. Schönberg, having exhausted his own anguish and fright, which were his only basis for musical imagery, moved in the middle 1920's to pure formalism. He contrived

---

* A glaring example of a disguised borrowing of an old work may be found by comparing the slow movement, "arioso," of Stravinsky's Concerto for Strings in D with Verdi's Prelude to Act I of *La Traviata*.

his "twelve-tone system" of musical composition, laying down more complicated and mechanistic rules for constructing a musical work than had been found in the knottiest products of Renaissance and Reformation counterpoint. A typical statement of principles is the following: "The development of music is more dependent than any other upon the development of its techniques. . . . An idea in music consists principally in the relation of tones to one another. But every relationship that has been used too much, no matter how extensively modified, must finally be regarded as exhausted; it ceases to have the power to convey a thought worthy of expression. Therefore the composer is obliged to invent new things, to present new relationships for discussion and to work out their consequences."[5] Thus, to Schönberg ideas no longer are to come out of the discovery of real events and relationships in a real world, but are a mystical property of musical tones. It is as if English-speaking writers were to proclaim not that they lacked ideas, but that the language was "exhausted." Their barrenness is not their fault but that of the dictionary. Stravinsky announced the liberating virtues of being in a formal prison: "The more I limit my field of action and hem myself in with obstacles, the greater and wider is my freedom. If I remove something that is hindering me, I am the weaker by its absence."[6] This is the opposite of the discipline of the realist, who finds the laws he must obey in faithfulness to reality and in the discovery of the constantly changing and unfolding movement of life. Again Stravinsky, who once proclaimed that music was "powerless to express anything at all,"[7] discovered and embraced the "unconscious." He wrote of his Symphony in Three Movements, composed during the second World War, "But during the process of creation in this arduous time of sharp and shifting events, of despair and hope, of continuous torments, of tension, and, at last, cessation and relief, it may be said that all these repercussions have left traces in this symphony. It is not for me to judge."[8] One can hardly imagine Mozart or Beethoven thus abandoning all claim to a conscious mind. And there is no better example of the degeneration of musical thought in the United States than the fact that such nonsensical statements as the above are reprinted and discussed with awe, like pronouncements of an oracle.

What is almost laughable about the proclamations of the "advanced" theoreticians about "new languages" is the fact that the actual music they produce is so musty. It scavenges in the past not in any sense of learning usable lessons, but by taking chunks of it over wholesale, and disguising it by a process similar to that of a distorting mirror. This sort of musical scavenging had already been apparent in much of Stravinsky's and Schönberg's music. The dead end has been reached with the appearance of the Schillinger system, replete with mathematical graphs and equations, which enable the student to take any musical work from the past, and so to alter its rhythmic patterns or harmonic scheme that it emerges seemingly new, although the listener finds it hard to explain the boredom that such "new" works inevitably engender. It was Schillinger's boast that he could turn out composers "like engineers." The system is taught in a number of music schools and the music departments of universities. It serves alike the composers of "advanced" works for festivals of "contemporary music" and the contrivers of Tinpan Alley "popular" songs. Tinpan Alley is today a beehive of disguised plagiarism, feeding on "classical" music, the improvised folk music of the Negro people, world folk music, and its own successful song "hits" of past decades.

In both the atonal and polytonal schools song forms and melody tend to disappear, both in writing for the voice and in providing an imagery for large-scale instrumental composition. Of course, modern theory claims that any succession of notes in time is "melody." The truth is, however, that song and the imagery connected with it are socially created, not arbitrarily invented; and the composer who does not provide melody that his listeners will regard as meaningful and close to them, has nothing with which to replace this lack. Both the atonal and polytonal composers end up with a form of writing much like the old "recitative" or song-speech, but lacking its socially created and moving melodic phrases. To the atonal composers, such as Schönberg and Berg, this speech in tone is the final refinement in dissonance, producing tones that are beyond the strictly musical. At the same time the instrumental accompaniment, as in Schönberg's song cycle, "Pierrot Lunaire," and Berg's opera, *Wozzeck,* consists of what can be analyzed on paper as all sorts of complicated contrapuntal forms, such as canons, fugues, passacaglias. But these forms are not designed to be followed by the ear and the mind. In classical music, form was meant to be consciously followed, not in technical terms but in its outline and movement, being the repository of conscious thought. To the "modern" this is turned upside down. The form is deliberately contrived not to be heard, like a carefully manufactured mental "unconscious," below the level of conscious perception yet controlling the music like a straitjacket.

To the impressionist and polytonal composers, this song-speech represents a dwindling of music back to its "pure" and primitive state, the intensification of declamation. The instrumental accompaniment is designed to enrich the speech intonations, giving them instrumental echoes. However, this reduction of music to the support and embodiment not of the meaning of speech but of its sounds alone, is not progress; it is a loss of crucial musical tools. In both kinds of music, the atonal and polytonal, the craftsmanship is frequently tremendous, but it is applied only to the end of producing an effect like primitive rituals. And the countless books and articles that theorize about this music provide no clarification, but only reveal a crisis of musical theory. Special pleadings for one narrow school or another are disguised as general theories of music, and the entire past history of music is transformed into a prelude to and justification for a present clique.

This question remains: If the "advanced" subjectivist and formalist schools are so foreign to real life and people's needs, why do they produce such excitement and rapture among the groups of composers and critics who cluster about them today? It is ironic that so much activity has developed about these schools precisely when both have become corpses, musically speaking. The reason is partly that these schools, for all their assumption of "rebellion," are the academicism of today, and academicism is always popular with conservative minds who want to be on the safe, or reactionary side of a cultural and social question. It is partly that these schools, with their elaborate formal systems, provide a means through which the composer can turn out a flock of works, each seemingly "well made" and praised by his fellow composers belonging to the same school, without having to embark on the strenuous activity of engaging in the struggles of real life and trying to reflect them in music. It is partly that these schools represent a world view, and enable the bourgeois who feels lost, afflicted by fears and torments, to make this fear and sense of doom into a philosophic generalization, seemingly true for all humanity. It is partly that formalism provides a means through which art can be made a substitute for life. The composer and listener find thrill and excitement in the sheer visceral impact and tensions of rhythm and timbre, in the shock quality of dissonant sounds. The conflicts rejected from life are replaced by the thrilling adventures of a flute and a trumpet, or of one tone with another. To composers and critical apologists for this kind of music, such compositions as those of Ernest Bloch, Ralph Vaughan-Williams, Jan Sibelius, and Sergei Rachmaninoff, which attempted to keep alive the tradition of dramatic, human, and folk-inspired music, with varying success, seem inexpressibly dull and obnoxious. Like merchants with a line of goods, they must deride this "rival" music to sell their own product. And of course any musical work or critical discussion of music that emanates from the Soviet Union is greeted with most virulent and irrational expressions of hatred. They sometimes pretend sympathy with the "criticized" Soviet composers, although the most "criticized" Soviet composer gets more performances of his music, and has more freedom actually to compose music, than the dozen most prominent composers in the United States put together. They deride Soviet music as "backward," "old-fashioned," "bourgeois," although wherever it has had a chance to be heard, it has become the most popular music with audiences because of the freshness and vitality of its human imagery. And typical of the degeneration of musical theory and criticism in the United States is that composers, theorists, and scholars, while avidly studying such areas of music as fourteenth century plain chant, show not the slightest interest in rediscovering and appraising the great traditions of the United States itself, such as the wealth of music that accompanied the working class struggles of the nineteenth century, or the phenomenal contributions of the Negro people.

9. *Music and Socialism*

THE REALISM OF OUR TIME must be based on the world view of the working class. Throughout the past, the working people who produced the necessities of life, first on the land and then in mine, shop, and factory, have been denied the means to develop themselves artistically. The common people have produced the wonders of folk art. But folk art was always a limited art, in the sense that the people were denied the possession of the most developed knowledge, techniques, and forms of art. These, like all education, were kept in the possession of the class which also owned the means of production.

Thus the progress of music in the past has been great but uneven. Shifts in social forces have been necessary for music to take a forward leap in content and form, to reach a new level of realism in description of life. And progress, although real, has always been onesided. The rise of the professional musician, a necessary step, meant the decline of the amateur and the popular participant. The rise of composition meant the decline of improvisation. The development of the great urban art of music in big composed forms was accompanied by the decline of folk music. Under capitalism, symphony and opera, chamber music and symphony are commercial and esthetic rivals; the skilled concert performer becomes the enemy of the composer, and the classics of the past are made to compete with the compositions of the present. With the exception of some slight remnants of feudal patronage in the form of gifts, grants, and prizes, music, both "classical" and "popular" music, both the concert hall and the writing of songs and dances for popular use, have become a business. The form and content of the music are controlled by the hirer of talents. These talents, however skilled, have to obey a dictation which disguises itself in the form of "box office" and profits. The "art for art's sake" rebel finds himself cut off contact with the people. The great mass of people are impelled to forget their own creativity, to become passive purchasers of a standardized, manufactured commodity.

Today the world is at the dawn of an unprecedented change, when the exploitation of one class by another will be abolished. The possibilities of man's collective mastery over nature, and ability to produce his needs from it, have developed to so great an extent that all people will be able to enjoy the fruits of their labor, not only in the sense of things consumed but in the sense of being able to develop their artistic powers to the fullest. This does not mean a "leveling." It means that far richer resources of artistic creation will be tapped than could ever have been tapped before. It means that mankind as a whole will have no other interest than knowing and mastering the world as a whole, without reservation or deviation from truth and reality due to class interests. This is the world view of the working class, which has no interest in exploiting others, or in anything but the truth of things as they are.

The breakdown of one-sidedness, to the end that all people may have the right and ability to develop their artistic talents; the fullest humanity, with no reservations; scientific knowledge of the forces, natural, economic, social, and historical, operating in the contemporary world; the partisanship on the side of progress—these may be called, in general, the content and goal of socialist realism.

In a considerable section of the world, working class societies, either socialist or moving directly toward socialism, now exist. This is a central historical fact of our time, and it must be understood by all people, whatever land they live in and whatever social class they belong to. The cause of peace as against the terrible destructiveness of another world war, the future of humanity itself, rests on the guarantee that socialism and capitalism will work out their future peacefully. Those who cannot see this, who speak of the "inevitability of war," or who take roundabout ways of saying the same thing by declaring that war is "deep in the human heart," "war is human nature," the human race is "doomed," or capitalism is synonymous with all "freedom" and "culture," and yet offer to lead or enlighten others, give up the right to be considered minds worthy of respect. From such frightened, ignorant, and poverty-stricken mentalities, such shrunken world views, no worthwhile, realist art can come.

What are the problems of socialist realist music today? One composer of our time demands some examination, for he represents the powerful struggle for a meaningful and progressive music on a base that was essentially not working class—the Hungarian Bela Bartok (1881-1945). He turned for inspiration to the peasantry. He said, "It [peasant music] is the ideal starting point for a musical renaissance, and a composer cannot be led by a better master." He devoted much of his life work to the collection and study of folk music, embracing the entire Balkans. His collection of over ten thousand folk songs is a permanent contribution to musical knowledge, and his many works of instruction based on folk material trace the rise of harmonic, polyphonic, and rhythmic patterns from their simplest beginnings. He carried on this work almost single-handed, sometimes with meager support from the Hungarian authorities and sometimes in the face of their hostility. His discoveries exploded many racist and chauvinist theories of musical origins, revealing the mixture of many strains that went to make a great folk culture. Yet in his search for the roots of folk music there lay the danger of taking too primitivist a view of folk music itself, denying its full song structures. And his intellectual life suffered from the false upholding of the countryside against the city, separating the peasantry from the city folk.

His large-scale works, such as his string quartets, sonatas, suites, and concertos, are developments of the forms, styles of instrumentation, and melodic material discovered in folk music. They are composed with great imagination, originality, and integrity. Yet the question arises of why this music should often sound so forbidding to the listener, so secretive, so harsh in its percussive sounds and over-complicated in its formal patterns. For all its human imagery, it also has much of an archaic quality. There is a disparity between sounds that would fit a folk improvisation, and the same sounds when they make up practically the entire texture of quartet, sonata, or concerto. His turn to the peasantry was productive of far richer experiences than Schönberg's or Stravinsky's turn to automatism, the "unconscious," or the abstract manipulation of musical tones. His music, especially between 1915 and 1920, reflects the deeply tragic experiences of the Hungarian and all the Balkan peasantry, used as cannon fodder in the first World War and betrayed afterward. And because he could see no way out for the peasantry, his music reached extremes of horror and violent feelings. Yet he never lost a sense of struggle and a feeling of healthy joy in life. At the same time, because he attempted to place so great a weight of musical structure and so much dramatic breadth upon the "pure" material of peasant music, this most earthy material became transformed in his music into a most personal and subjective imagery. His progress was slow and tortuous. Although, unlike the extremists, he never discarded theoretically the great classic and realistic heritage of the past, it was only near the end of his life that he began successfully to attain some of these qualities in large-scale works —his Concerto for Orchestra, for example. And his comparative failure indicates that the problem of a realistic and progressive musical culture today could not be solved by one man in isolation, and with so comparatively great an abandonment of the best skills of the past.

The working class approach to music combines the humanity of folk music, the continual search for genuine human imagery born out of the people's life and struggles against oppression, with the techniques to be learned from the cumulative developments of musical realism. It seeks both an art of daily use and one presenting the richest and broadest dramatic and social experiences. In working class countries, music like all art is removed from the competitiveness of the private market place, just as it is also removed from the remnants of private patronage. Music is supported by the great mass of people, and this is guaranteed by making it easily available to them. It is as much their right as the right to work, and as available as bread. Symphonic concerts, opera, chamber music organizations, have no trouble in existing. They are part of the social services of the community, and expand in numbers as rapidly as they can be organized and trained. Constant education is carried on by presenting the masterworks of the past, and there is no end to the demand for fresh works of the present. The people, for the first time, can really support the composer. And at the same time, there is a great expansion of amateur music-making, of singing and instrumental performance groups, which in itself is a rich musical education for the people taking part.

In the Soviet Union, for example, during the earliest years, when the country was ravaged by invasion and by civil war financed and sustained by the imperialist powers, the greatest attention was given to the building and preservation of culture. During the whole growth of the Soviet Union, constant attention was given to the development of the arts, including music, not merely in "expressions of interest" but in the most material way, in the allotment of as great a part of each year's budget as was possible to the building of theaters, conservatories, opera companies, orchestras, and the manufacture of musical instruments. In 1939, 29 new operas by Soviet composers were produced. During a typical music season, such as that of 1940-41, a new opera by Khrennikov received 154 performances in 26 theaters. Other new operas by Soviet composers received respectively 130, 39, 34, and 34 performances.

There has been a constant fostering of the cultures of the national republics and autonomous national groups, with a drive on the one hand to preserve and encourage their traditional folk cultures, and on the other to introduce symphonic and opera forms hitherto unknown to these peoples. There are periodic gala festivals of folk music in the major cities, with performers coming from every corner of the Soviet Union. New forms are developed, such as a kind of opera which combines folk with standard concert instruments, and composed music with improvisation. As one example of such national development, the people of Buryat Mongolia, who in 1929 did not know symphonic and opera music, were, in 1940, able to send a complete ballet and opera company to Moscow, for a fortnight of Buryat Mongolian musical art. Composers have organized themselves into a union, similar to writers' and painters' unions, which fixes rates of compensation and royalties, carries on musical education, fosters musical composition, subsidizes young and rising composers. Musical education for children is especially rich, both as a normal part of schooling and in the form of Schools for Specially Talented Musical Children. There no talented musical performer ever has a problem of making a living, and the demand far exceeds the numbers available. When an important new composition is being prepared for performance, articles describing it fill a great deal of the space in the daily newspapers. In 1946, while the people were repairing the ravages of the Nazi invasion, plans were announced for training 39 new symphony orchestras, as well as a large number of choruses and chamber music groups.

The effect of such a musical life upon the composer can be seen in

the career of Dmitri Shostakovich. Born in 1906, he began his professional musical studies under the bleak conditions of 1919 in what is
now Leningrad. He graduated from the conservatory in 1923, and two
years later completed his First Symphony, which won great acclaim
both in the Soviet Union and throughout Europe and the United
States. It is a remarkable work in its grasp of the essential dramatic
and large-scale character of the symphony form, its warm lyricism and
absolute clarity of expression, true to the great humanist Russian
musical tradition. At the same time it is wholly fresh and modern,
with a brilliant use of orchestral color, a wry dissonance punctuating
the melodies, and a roguish humor.

His work of the next few years was not on the level of the First
Symphony. The scathing criticism received by his opera, *Lady Macbeth
of Mtsensk,* in 1936, was widely publicized throughout Europe and
the United States, with no attempt to understand it. There were dire
predictions as to what would happen to Shostakovich and to Soviet
music, predictions which the developments of the next few years
showed to be absolutely ridiculous. Shostakovich remained a highly
respected teacher and composer. During the 1920's and early 1930's,
however, Soviet musicians had avidly welcomed and studied the "advanced" music of Europe, with many performances of operas and
symphonic scores by Berg, Hindemith, Milhaud, and others. Many
composers fell into the trap of believing that a "revolutionary" and
"people's" music would be achieved by abandoning the entire classic
past, standing it on its head, writing exclusively witty, satiric, and
nose-thumbing works, or naturalistic noises representing locomotives
and factories. These manacles on musical development were broken
by the criticism of *Lady Macbeth of Mtsensk.*

Soviet criticism is no dogmatic statement "from above," nor is it
an "order," as the American press has so loudly proclaimed. It is an
attempt by leading figures in Soviet political and cultural life to formu-
late consciously and clearly the needs, reactions, and thinking of the
people themselves, to represent a "social consciousness," an awareness
of realities that are otherwise expressed through people's simply
staying away from music. It is an effort to provide a means through
which leading artists and the people can be brought closer together,
and thus to provide the only means through which the artist himself

can grow. The criticism of 1936 was a restatement of the fundamental principles of Soviet cultural life, the need to master and reshape critically the best achievements of the past, and to foster an art capable of representing contemporary life.

The proof of the value of the criticisms is seen in the music itself. The works of Shostakovich that were criticized, such as his *Golden Age* ballet music and *Lady Macbeth,* along with similar works like Mossolov's *Iron Foundry,* are well known, and there is no avid desire anywhere to revive them. They are technically brilliant, with much satiric humor, but they are at the same time flimsy music, with much of the thin and negative quality found in the "disillusioned" music of the twenties. They lack human imagery, and represent a "revolutionary" music from which the people stay away in droves, feeling that they themselves are being laughed at.

The Fifth Symphony, which Shostakovich wrote in 1936-37, was a work such as no one could have told him to write. It was a re-creation of the qualities of the First Symphony with a new breadth and maturity. Again the quality of the work is proven by its reception. It has become one of the few symphonies of this century which have established themselves as a permanent part of the concert repertory, deeply loved by people the world over and turned to again and again. The Fifth Symphony does have a genuinely new style in the only real meaning of the term, clear and expressive and yet characteristic of the composer, like nothing else being written. Typical of this forward stride is the first movement, which is lucid, intensely human and expressive, without an ounce of padding. A long, continuous melodic declamation in "arioso" style, it combines melodic phrases with poignant speech-like intonations and with an inexpressibly moving dramatic and tragic quality.

Along with this expressive declamatory style, which also appears in the opening movement of the Sixth Symphony and the slow movement of the Seventh, "Leningrad," Symphony, Shostakovich also showed himself to be a melodist of the most ingratiating quality, full of both a boisterous "popular" humor, as in the finale of his Fifth and Sixth symphonies, and a quiet charm, as in the Quintet for Piano and Strings. The problem he next faced was that of attaining an even richer and deeper musical style by uniting song-like melody and its

human images with the most intensely dramatic texture. He made
a great step in this direction with his "Leningrad" Symphony. This
work, written while he was taking part in the defense of Leningrad
in the first months of the fascist invasion, is a historic achievement
of twentieth century music. Moving audiences deeply throughout
the anti-fascist world, the work was a triumph of music itself, making the art as meaningful and exciting to people, through purely
musical means, as their daily newspaper. It proved that music was
far from "effete" or esoteric, that it could be of the utmost importance
to people's lives, inspiring them in their collective struggle against
the forces of reaction and human destruction.

The career of Sergei Prokofiev reveals equally well, although in
a different way, the fruitful relations of an artist to socialist society.
Born in 1891, by the time of the Revolution of 1917 he was a fully
formed composer. Like most "young progressives" of his generation,
he had been brought up to regard all nineteenth century musical style
with horror, while wit and satire remained the weapons of the "future."
Yet, in spite of this narrow esthetic, his early works, such as the
"Classical" Symphony, the "Fugitive Visions," and the First Violin
Concerto had a loveliness of melody that lifted them far above the
ruck of "modernist" music. In 1918 he left the Soviet Union, returned
for a visit in 1927, then went to Paris again to work with Diaghilev,
the ballet producer who was sponsoring Stravinsky. His music of the
late twenties and early thirties indicates clearly and conclusively how
his talents were beginning to degenerate, and the kind of blind alley in
which he was in danger of ending. It was a blind alley which few
of his colleagues escaped. Some of the works of this period are the
Quintet for Wind and Strings, Opus 39; the ballet, *Age of Steel;* the
Divertimento, Opus 43. They are terribly thin music, tending to be
dominated by instrumental timbres and a mechanical rhythm.

In 1932 he returned to the Soviet Union to stay; and gradually a
completely new period in his music began to take shape. Not only was
there a greater richness and depth of melody, but the entire make-up
of his work showed the influence of living in the Soviet Union. His
great evening-long ballet, *Romeo and Juliet,* reflected the love of the
people for Shakespeare, and their insistence on a human and social understanding of the drama. His "Alexander Nevsky" Cantata, written

for an Eisenstein film, in its pictorial quality, dramatic feeling, and folk quality reflected the realistic Soviet approach to history, unfolding the role played by the common people. His Fifth Symphony should really have been called his first, in the sense that it was his first to seek the epic heroic and philosophical character without which a symphony is only a travesty of the form. His Sonata in F Minor for violin and piano, Opus 80, was a deeply moving war work, and one of the most dramatic works in this form of the entire century. In late years he has written a number of ballets which have been warmly received, but which have not been heard on these shores.

In the Soviet Union, criticism is a sign of the high regard the people have for music and its creators. This will seem especially strange to composers in the United States who regard critics as arch-enemies except when they themselves become critics. Yet the proof of the regard lies in the high position Shostakovich has always held in Soviet musical life, in the fact that his melodies are hummed by millions, in the fact that his successful symphonic works are known by music lovers as thoroughly as they know the great classics. The Soviet criticisms are part of the flourishing musical life of the country, of the give and take between artist and people. They are part of the process through which the composer is made aware of the progress of the people themselves, and the need to catch up with them and at the same time give them a consciousness of their being through his work that they could not attain by themselves. Through these criticisms Shostakovich has grown, as few other composers in these difficult times. His deeply moving expressions of pain and tragedy, his joyfulness and impish humor have become a world cultural possession. This growth is true of other Soviet composers; and in general, Soviet music as a whole, in spite of red-baiting, has become the most popular body of contemporary music. It is popular in the real sense of the term, not the commercial best-seller sense, which creates works to be consumed and destroyed so that they may make room for others. It is turned to again and again. Not every work is a masterpiece, but every work is human, and the listeners feel in the music a deep regard for themselves.

One of the effects of the Soviet criticisms has been to puncture the carefully nurtured myths about "modernism" in music, myths so well publicized that the listeners who felt only boredom, distaste, or confusion at this music began to feel that the fault was in their own lack of "finer sensitivities." The Soviet Union has raised questions of music, asking that it possess not only "talent," or cleverness, or experimental novelty, but seriousness and depth. This, too, has been well expressed by Shostakovich, on his visit to the United States in 1949 as a delegate to the Cultural and Scientific Conference for World Peace. "Bringing into being a work which must be permeated with great ideas and great passions, which must convey with its sounds tragic suspense as well as deep optimism, and must reaffirm the beauty and dignity of man—this is the difficult and complicated task which realism demands."[1] And the great power of realism is that it enables the composer himself to be a powerful factor for peace against war. And so Shostakovich asks, "How can we musicians serve the cause of peace, democracy and progress with our art?"

The criticisms and discussions of 1948 were again derided throughout the capitalist world by composers and critics, especially in the United States, along with a fury of Soviet-baiting and dire predictions of the imminent collapse of Soviet music. And while writing these attacks in the name of the "freedom" of the composer to compose music, these same composers were worrying about when they could find some spare time to compose, how they could make some money out of their composition, and why nobody seemed either to like their music or even to be interested in their existence. Needless to say, these critics and "authorities" have made no attempt to prove or disprove their predictions by examining the new works of Soviet music, such as Shostakovich's "Song of the Forest," a cantata for chorus and orchestra on a grand scale, with a rich and fresh melodic quality, celebrating in words and music peaceful life and construction. It is one of the few really "new" works of the postwar years, for it deals with the vistas opening up before humanity after the defeat of fascism. And the music fits the subject, having a lyric sweetness and a joyousness surpassing everything in his previous work.

The criticism of 1948, which inaugurated widespread discussions by composers, musicians, critics, and the public, was aimed at accelerating the development of Soviet music by making the composers aware of the vast changes that had taken place among the people, the new avenues of musical composition that were opening up, the new needs of the people. It laid the basis for a new level of socialist realism, breaking down all previous opposition that had existed between concert hall and opera, between music for professional and music for amateur, between instrumental music and vocal, between music of the most serious "classical" principles and music for popular use. It pointed out that Soviet music had developed one-sidedly, in its attention to the concert hall; that the tens of thousands of amateur choral and instrumental groups offered Soviet composers great opportunities for reaching audiences far beyond the concert hall, providing the people with music of the best quality, and raising their level; and that this effort would in turn, enable the composer to develop new resources of human imagery in music. It called for a serious and far deeper approach to the problems of opera than had been made hitherto, pointing out that Soviet composers had suffered from the failing to write for the human voice and the neglect of vocal music and song, characteristic of the decline of bourgeois music in general. One of the profound remarks made by Andrei A. Zhdanov (1896-1948) in his speech at a conference of Soviet musicians was as follows: "I shall now pass on to the danger of losing professional mastery. If formalistic distortions make music poorer, they also entail another danger: the loss of professional mastery. In this connection it would be well to consider still another widespread misconception: the claim that classical music is supposedly simpler, and modern music more complex, and the complexity of modern music represents a forward step."[2] This is true of a great number of contemporary composers, who speak in mysterious shop-talk terms of their "advanced" techniques, when they have actually lost basic skills, such as those of constructing a large-scale dramatic work, writing an opera that presents credible human characterizations on the stage, or even writing a genuinely emotional and singable melody.

Opera happens to be one of the richest of historic musical forms, capable of both the greatest music and the greatest popularity, educating people in the meaning of all music by associating music with dramatic events and experiences. Like all forms of theater, it has been feared and censored by reactionary governments, and it is significant that the Soviet criticisms call for even more intensive work on opera, and a devotion to the most real and contemporary themes. The criticism attacks narrowness and calls for more breadth, for "works of high quality and high ideals in all genres—in the field of operatic and symphonic music, in the creation of songs, in choral and dance music."

The criticism touches on other points that could well be examined in the United States: the charge, for example, that music criticism "has made itself a trumpet for individual composers. Some music critics have taken to fawning upon one or another of the leading musicians, praising their works, in every way, for reasons of friendship, rather than criticizing them on the basis of objective principles." The cliquishness dominating the circles in which contemporary music is discussed in the United States, is obvious to anyone who has contact with them.

Zhdanov called for more "creative discussion," saying: "When there is no creative discussion, no criticism and self-criticism, there can be no progress either. . . . When criticism and creative discussion are lacking, the wellsprings of growth run dry, and a hothouse atmosphere of stuffiness and stagnation is created."[3] Self-criticism is nothing new in musical history. Every great artist has gone through periods of deep self-examination, harshly criticizing his previous work and trying to discover new pathways to growth. The new aspect of Soviet criticism is that it is more open, social, and collective, more conscious of the historical forces that in fact have always forwarded the progress of music. Again Zhdanov said: "Not everything that is comprehensible is a work of genius, but every genuine work of genius is comprehensible, and it is all the more a work of genius, the more comprehensible it is to the broad masses of people." This is a restatement of nothing more than what the history of music displays, for Bach, Mozart, Beethoven, Verdi, Tchaikovsky were comprehended in their time, within the limits of the audiences they could reach. It does not say that all great music is immediately comprehended by all listeners. It says that great art can be explained and taught, and to claim that today's art will be understood only by the "future" is to hide its poverty-stricken content.

Again Zhdanov declared: "Internationalism arises from the very flowering of national art. To forget this truth is to lose sight of the guiding line, to lose one's own face, to become a homeless cosmopolitan. Only the nation which has its own highly developed musical culture can appreciate the music of other peoples. One cannot be an internationalist in music, or in any other realm, without being at the same time a genuine patriot of one's own country. If internationalism is founded on respect for other peoples, one cannot be an internationalist without respecting and loving one's own people."[4] This too is worthy of study by many composers in the United States, who produce a music according to an atonal or polytonal set of formulas that is exactly like the music produced by the same formulas in Paris, Vienna, London, and Rome, and which is profoundly boring to audiences both abroad and at home. Internationalism is the mutual help and interchange of ideas, experiences and knowledge among peoples. Cosmopolitanism is the attempted dictatorship of a dominant imperialist culture over peoples through the insistence on musical systems that preclude realism or human imagery, and which destroy national cultures wherever their influence is felt. Today the cosmopolitan dictatorship of atonality and polytonality, and of the manufactured music of Tinpan Alley, go hand in hand, and their destructive influence is easy to see, both in Europe and in the United States itself.

An example of how little these criticisms are understood is provided by Nicholas Slonimsky, in an article called "The Change in Styles of Soviet Music," printed in the *Journal of the American Musicological Society*. This article is full of discoveries of "retarding tendencies" in Soviet music, consisting of statements by Soviet composers promising to produce "vivid realistic music that reflects the life and struggles of the Soviet people," and recognizing "the imperative necessity to activate in every way the artistic and musical education of the masses."[5] Would, one wonders, a statement by a group of American composers that they aimed at a "vivid, realistic music that reflects the life and struggles of the American people," or a program to improve "the artistic and musical education of the American people," be considered a retarding tendency?

10. *Music in the United States*

TODAY IN EVERY COUNTRY the task facing the composer, for the sake of his own future, is to fight for a peaceful world, for friendship and understanding among peoples, and to try to create a music of strong human imagery and realistic dramatic content, understandable to the listeners and able to move them. He must fight for the right to be able to use every possible form—the symphonic, the operatic, the song and dance—against the barrier of the commercialism which runs the concert stage and the "popular" music world alike. A potential audience for the arts exists today, as well as a reservoir of creative talent, of a kind unknown at any previous period. All cultural barriers that held sway in the past, such as those between the culture of the slave-owners and the slaves, between the feudal manors and the peasant folk, between the city and the countryside, have become archaic. The artist has the power to move people, and thus to accelerate the forward movement of history itself, to an extent unknown at any previous time. This perspective and possibility mean also that the reactionary pressures upon the artist to ignore the real world and the life of his fellow human beings become the fiercer. The extent to which anti-realist trends become dominant in a country's culture is a sign of how fierce these pressures are.

The cultural life of Nazi Germany was a prime example of such flight from reality. A façade of demands for a "volk" culture and attacks on "modernism" was thrown up. But "volk" culture meant not a turn to the people of the present, but a reversion to the worst superstition and violence that could be dredged up from primitive tribal practices. Despite attacks on "modernism," Stravinsky's polytonal and visceral music, Richard Strauss's violent dissonances and blood-drenched treatment of old legends became wholly acceptable. Wagner's

106

Nibelungen legends and his anti-Semitism became the high point of all musical culture, and even Bach's *St. Matthew Passion* was exploited for the anti-Semitism that had lingered in this version of the medieval passion play. The greatest conductors and musical performers were driven out of the country. Creative composition came to an end. There was a rising market in pornographic songs. Not one musical work of any real quality or human appeal came out of these dozen years. Even today, in Western Germany, a correspondent of the *New York Times* writes, in this case of literature: "The Germans have gone in for a blend of the Nibelungen legends with the Krupp works."[1]

There is nothing in the past of United States music comparable to the place in our culture of the poetry of Whitman, or the novels of Cooper, Hawthorne, Melville, Mark Twain, and Dreiser. This does not mean that the people are unmusical. The United States has one of the richest bodies of folk music in the world, brought by people from every corner of the earth, the music crisscrossing and sending out fresh shoots. Like all folk music, it has flourished most and sent out new greenery when used as a vital part of the people's labor, social life, and struggle. There were large bodies of songs of the Revolutionary War, songs of the War of 1812, sea chanteys, "mechanics'" songs which reflected the early organization struggles of American labor, Civil War songs, mine, lumber camp, and railroad ballads, trade union songs.

The greatest creative contribution to United States folk music was made by the Negro people. A rich heritage was brought from Africa, representative of the cultures which were being devastated by the slave trade. This African musical heritage, absorbing the words and music of the hymns found on American soil, produced the wonderful body of spirituals, which rose between 1830 and 1860 as a powerful weapon of the struggle against slavery. They were a means for affirming solidarity among the Negro people, Underground Railroad signals and messages, and battle songs; a religious music of a people to whom a religion was meaningful only as it supported the struggle against slavery in the real world. Just as the anti-slavery struggle was a historic step in the progress and democratization of the country as a whole, so the spirituals have become the best-loved body of folk music among all the people, although many people, even when moved by the strength and beauty of the spirituals, are unaware of the nature of the struggles which produced them.

The great body of American popular song and dance music, the music today associated with Tinpan Alley, has at its core the creative contribution of the Negro people. A formalistic factory-manufactured music, as the great mass of Tinpan Alley music is, cannot invent. It must borrow, steal, plagiarize, and formalize its material from some-where. Tinpan Alley today borrows from everywhere, Grieg and Tchaikovsky, Mexican tangos and songs from every national group, cowboy and mountain songs. However, the turns of melody, the rhythms and instrumentation that are most characteristically "American" in sound, are taken from the secular songs and dances, both improvised and composed, of the Negro people.

This secular music took shape in the days of plantation slavery, in the form of labor songs, field calls, and dances like the cakewalk, which were satiric of the slave-owners. In the closing decades of the nineteenth century and the first decades of the twentieth, there grew up the rich ballad music of the blues, and also, in the Negro communities of the Southern waterfront and river cities, such as Savannah, St. Louis, Mem-phis, and New Orleans, a remarkable instrumental music called rags or ragtime. This instrumental music was largely march and dance, but, in its formal organization and polyphonic interweaving of melodic lines, it went far beyond ordinary dance needs. It used instruments taken over from military bands, such as trumpet, clarinet, and trom-bone. The music was suffused with rich melodic and song-speech qualities, carrying a freight of human images of past and present life and struggles. It profited from both the folk tradition and the mastery of violin, piano, and other instruments that the Negro people had shown, serving in the ballrooms of wealthy white people.

Between 1900 and 1930 a number of creative personalities appeared, such as Scott Joplin, Ferdinand Morton, Joseph Oliver, Bessie Smith, Lillian Hardin, William Handy, and Louis Armstrong. Their music still used traditional folk patterns, but it attained qualities not found in any previous folk music. It had a wealth of personal invention and expression, a musical knowledge, an exciting interchange of ideas between one musician and another, which brought it to the border of what may be called a composed "art" music. These singers, instrumentalists, and song writers had the ability to become leading American composers, granted rational and humane conditions to develop their talents. They were regarded, however, as "entertainers" in the sleaziest sense of the word, having to work for the most part for white audiences who treated them with vilest chauvinism, and often forced them to assume a clown role in order to exist as musicians.

It has always been true of folk music, and was true of jazz, that the very rudimentary nature of the materials the folk had to use, the double-meaning, secretive language, enabled this art to be formalized and transformed into a grotesque attack upon the folk themselves. Thus the minstrel shows of the mid-nineteenth century, presented by white entertainers in black face, were a grotesque perversion of Negro music. Similarly jazz, as it developed commercially, took its strength and fresh ideas from this Negro music, and then formalized it, transforming it into a perversion of the original, emphasizing the outer shell and lifting it out of its social setting. The 1910's and 1920's were the period in which the publication of "popular" music was growing from small business to big, and was still open to fresh invention. Many songs by Negro composers became highly popular, innumerable other songs were "arranged," without credit, from Negro music, and the leading white composers, like George Gershwin, Hoagy Carmichael, Vincent Youmans, and Richard Rodgers, were deeply influenced by the Negro music. The popular songs of this period, although they already show the standardized Tinpan Alley straitjacket of form and the censored, inane words characteristic of all "popular" published music, have not been surpassed since.

In the 1930's and 1940's popular song and dance music were linked to monopoly and became subservient to the great phonograph record companies, the cinema industry, and radio. Yet even in this period it was mainly Negro musicians, such as Edward Kennedy Ellington, William Basie, Theodore Wilson, and Mary Lou Williams who fought for their integrity as creative musicians, transforming jazz into as much of an art form as it could be within the limitations of a dance and a three-minute phonograph recording, and producing the thin stream of genuinely touching and beautiful music within the mountains of rubbish of commercial jazz. This was done in an environment where every fresh idea was regarded with hostility by the commercial managers, only to be stolen, formalized, and become the "hit" pattern of later years. And in this period the Negro musicians were the lowest paid, the most often unemployed, and in most cases segregated and with rare exceptions forbidden to perform with white musicians.

The question arises: If the United States has so rich a heritage of folk music, and if there is so much public musical activity, why has composed, "art" music been so weak and fragile a growth? The most common answer is to blame the people for the debasement of music by the "popular" factory-style music industry. Yet everything creative in this music came from the common people, and was understood and welcomed by the common people. The true reason appears when the conditions under which folk music grew are examined. It was always a music of struggle. This does not mean that it was only a direct attack upon oppressive political and social conditions, although it was this as well, for it reflected every side of life and personality. Among the Negro people, it was angry, satiric, and lamenting, and also full of gay humor and joy in life. It asserted the kinship of people and proved the existence of a growing national culture. It was a means through which the people could fight and also assert their right to love, to laughter, and to growth, a means through which they could affirm every side of their humanity, in the face of an oppressing class which tried to treat them as chattels and denied them the common rights of human beings. Fundamentally, and through a longer sweep of history, these have also been the conditions for the development of composed, "art" music, which has reflected and played a part in the rise of nations and produced the freshest musical ideas, as in the great operas, songs, and symphonies, when it took on the battle of ideas, the hammering out of new concepts of human personality and relationships, the world view of what was being born as against what was dying.

Musical composition in the United States has rarely been looked upon as such an arena of ideas and struggle. Concert music and opera were predominantly a luxury imported from Europe, patronized by the rich as a plaything and imitation of the European aristocracy, and kept largely for the rich. The wealthy patrons of opera never conceived of the idea of sponsoring a music drama with roots deep in American life and music.

There were some United States composers of the nineteenth century, however, who tried earnestly to create an American music. They saw the problem, however, as one of affixing vaguely "American" melodies to forms taken over bodily from the work of the "best" European composers. One of these Americans was Edward MacDowell (1861-1908), most of whose work is admirably and seriously put together and yet unmistakably dead. An example of his "American" music is an "Indian Suite." The themes are Indian, but they are used simply as exotic color. There is no attempt to portray in music the real life, character, and struggles of the Indian people and to see them as human beings.

A worthwhile American art had to be a democratic art. A democratic art had to be realistic. It had to be based on an understanding of the fact that, from its beginnings, the United States republic had been built on the despoiling of the Indian people, on slavery, and, after the Civil War, on semi-slavery and Jim Crow enforced by both law and lynch rope. Such art had to remove blinders from people's eyes. The great Czech composer, Anton Dvorak (1841-1904), when he visited the United States in the nineties, threw a bombshell into the musical world when he declared that the most beautiful American folk music he had heard, and a music most worthy of study and use by composers, was the body of Negro spirituals. The esthetes found it hard to assimilate the fact that the best American music had come from the slaves. A pupil of MacDowell, Henry F. Gilbert (1869-1928), wrote a "Comedy Overture on Negro Themes" and a ballet, *The Dance in the Place Congo,* using Negro music. Yet in these works also the Negro themes only added a sort of strange, exotic color. Both the tone of the music and the "programs" to which it is set resemble the kind of work which is becoming all too familiar—the bids to "befriend" the Negro people which are so misinformed, patronizing, and insulting that they might as well be the work of enemies. Probably the most successful of truly American composed music of the last century was a handful of piano pieces by Louis Moreau Gottschalk (1829-1869) on American Negro and West Indian themes. These compositions preserve a true folk character in their freshness of melody, rhythm, and texture. They treat their material with respect for its human character, and not as strangely interesting and novel sounds. Gottschalk, a Creole, was the great American pianist of his time.

The Metropolitan Opera House in New York is a typically feudal structure, built by the "robber barons" as a "society" toy. The company is not American, except that it saves money by teaching American singers to sing bad French, Italian, and German, nor is it even a true show-place or museum of the great classical heritage, for a host of masterpieces are never put on its boards. Symphony and opera are run by boards of wealthy dilettantes. Their seasons are short, and their prices of admission prohibitive to the great mass of people, if indeed the people are even within physical reaching distance of them. After the economic crash of 1929, the wealthy patrons of opera and symphony decided not even to pay the bills. While clinging to their patronage and grip over the policies of the organization, raising an outcry against any move to public sponsorship, they appealed to the public for donations in the name of preserving "culture."

Since 1900 there has been a steadily increasing amount of serious musical composition in the United States, giving the country at least the appearance of having an "art" music. And yet this musical life is beset by deep contradictions.

The greatest amount of public sponsorship of musical composition took place during the 1930's, in the form of work relief projects and the W.P.A. These produced some remarkable musical plays, composers' forum laboratories in which composers could discuss their work with the public, and inexpensive symphony concerts. The pro-labor movement and anti-fascist spirit of the times inspired ground-breaking works such as Earl Robinson's *Ballad for Americans* and Marc Blitzstein's *The Cradle Will Rock*. Researches of the most historic importance were undertaken on the wealth of American folk music. Yet all this was looked upon simply as "unemployment relief," and the door to the flowering of these great potentialities for musical life was soon slammed shut.

The United States, the foremost industrial power of the twentieth century, has led the world in the production of mechanical means for reproducing music—the radio, cinema, and phonograph record. This has undeniably helped the spread of musical education, and enabled large numbers of people to become familiar with the great classics of music in splendid performances. Yet this progress has taken place subject to the laws of market-place sale and profit and its brutal competitiveness, so that a gain in one direction is countered by destruction in another. All music becomes a luxury commodity, and one form of musical production must fight for its life against another, although all are necessary for a healthy and rounded musical life. The motion picture and radio, which represent the art avenues created by capitalism in its monopoly stage, have shown a complete disinterest in encouraging an American music of any kind. Hollywood and radio represent jazz at its worst, and have never recognized the dignity and true worth of the contribution of the Negro people. The radio programs are media for corporation advertising. Classical music appears in dribs and drabs and only if some great corporation decides it will help sell its product or gain it prestige. A composer who once had two operas produced at the Metropolitan Opera House, Deems Taylor, is today a radio "disc jockey," playing fragments of classical music.

Phonograph recordings have helped the spread of musical knowledge, and in their early days were a medium through which many of the great Negro jazz performers were able to develop their art. Yet in the competitive market-place world, the effect of the phonograph was not to increase interest and sponsorship of "live" music but to throw vast numbers of musicians out of employment. The musicians' union conducted bitter strikes against "canned" music, and today more than half of the union members are unemployed. Another effect of the mechanized production of music, and the transformation of music into a commercial commodity produced by professional skills, has been almost to kill amateur music and home music-making. The result is that a great source of potential creative talent, and a means for building the appreciation of music and developing the human imagery of music, is dried up. American performers find the road to growth almost prohibitively difficult, for the concert network of the entire country is controlled by two great management chains, which are affiliated to the two great phonograph companies and radio chains. These chains can make or break a performer, pay meagerly, dictate programs, and force the ambitious concert artist to give concerts at his or her own expense in the hope of making a reputation.

In the realm of musical composition, no serious composer can make a living out of his work. No money can be made from writing a full-scale opera, for the chance of public performance is so small, and the work demanded so great, aside from the fact that the composer cannot get the feel of working on the opera stage for live audiences. A symphony is performed generally after the composer has pulled the strings of society patronage, and even then the performance may cost the composer as much as a thousand dollars, for he must have the parts copied himself. The composer, Aaron Copland, has carried on a continuous and so far unsuccessful battle to organize composers so that they can gain some monetary return for their work. Concerts of contemporary American music are expensive to organize and cannot compete as commercial commodities with the concerts of the most highly publicized and dazzling performing artists. As a result, American composition is generally a kind of in-grown production offered to audiences of other composers, fashioned to meet their shop-talk and cliquish criticism. The vast amounts spent today for war production and the rising taxes and cost of living cut further into the minute sums in the public pocket available for the support of music. The slightest grant of government support to music is considered "socialistic." Ironically enough, large sums are spent so that the Voice of America can offer to Europe recordings and performances of American music, which the American public cannot hear, as a sign of the cultural life of the country. A concert conducted by the highly talented Dean Dixon, who cannot get a job with any United States symphony orchestra because he is a Negro, and sponsored by the Council on African Affairs, which is being attacked as "subversive," was recorded and produced in Europe by the Voice of America as an example of American musical culture. Paul Robeson, the great and beloved Negro artist, who decided to break with the concert world and to offer his talents to the masses of people who are outside the narrow and specialized concert audiences, is at this writing being hounded at his appearances at home and prevented from touring abroad.

The work of the leading twentieth century composers exhibits the destructive effect of the contradictions at the heart of the nation's musical life. The most original and in many ways profound of United States composers, Charles Ives (1874—), worked for almost all of his active career in complete isolation, his music never publicly performed but known only to himself and a few friends. The music is remarkable in its grand scale, its free and imaginative use of American popular idiom, such as hymn tunes, barn dances, street marches, popular songs, and ragtime, its attempt to re-create the great classic nineteenth century musical forms, to embody something of the communal spirit of "small-town" democracy, the Civil War debates and the populist spirit of the 1890's. It makes a bold effort to embody philosophic concepts in music, as in the "Concord Sonata" which tries, and with no mean success, to catch in music the personalities of Emerson, Hawthorne, the Alcotts, and Thoreau. Yet the lack of public performances had an almost disastrous effect on the composer, for much of the music is almost unplayable in its difficulty, and sometimes the actual sounds heard do not seem to carry out what the composer had in mind, for they emerge as harsh and incomprehensible. It is this destructive isolation of the composer—from criticism, from performances of his work, from money return, from any sign that people are interested in his existence—which the critic in the United States today hails as "freedom."

George Gershwin (1898-1937) had probably the richest melodic gift of any American composer. Yet his songs, most of them written for Broadway musical shows, suffer from the formalist Tinpan Alley pattern imposed on him, and the shallowness of the pseudo-poetry to which they are set. His "opera," *Porgy and Bess,* the music of which owes a great debt to Negro music, was a sorry attempt to romanticize life among the Negro poor. This work and his ambitious concert orchestral pieces also suffered from the fact that he could never break wholly away from the Tinpan Alley harmonic, instrumental and structural clichés.

Aaron Copland (1900—) is generally respected as the greatest master among United States composers, an artist of great integrity as a craftsman in every work he turns out. Copland studied music in Paris during the 1920's. There he was especially attracted to the school of thought which lumped together the classic heritage of Beethoven and the latest romanticism of Wagner as one great body of "outmoded" music, and hailed the "return" to the eighteenth century and to the artisan spirit of feudalism as "progress." The result is a narrowness of experience and range of feeling in his music, a tendency to let the instrumental sound dominate and thus constrict the entire musical conception, all in the name of "clarity" and "form." There seems to be a constant fear that to break out into a genuinely dramatic experience, to represent the real conflicts of life, to search for singing, lyrical qualities, would be thought "old-fashioned" and even vulgar by his fellow composers. Not only he but almost his entire generation of American composers, such as Roger Sessions, Roy Harris, Virgil Thomson, and Walter Piston, suffered from this fundamental error of regarding formalistic systems or a borrowing from feudalism as a "liberation" of American music. And today, the most powerful influences and admired teachers in the United States are such composers as Schönberg, Stravinsky, and Hindemith, who are violently opposed to any national and realistic qualities in music, seem to live in an intellectual world of the medieval past, teach completely formalist systems, and seem to think that emotions, if they enter music at all, do so through the "unconscious." This has become the pattern of the greatest part of musical composition in the United States today.

One of the destructive influences in United States cultural life has been the "melting pot" theory. The rapidly expanding industrialization made it necessary to attract great numbers of working people from other countries, and it was these people—the Irish, Italian, German, Slovak, Jewish from Central and Eastern Europe, Polish, Czech, Chinese, Mexican and others—whose labor, along with that of the Negro people, actually built the country. Yet it was necessary for these working people to be taught to "keep their place." The "melting pot" theory taught in the schools, proclaimed in the press, demanded that they be ashamed of their national cultural background and heritage, admiring as a "true" American type some mythical Anglo-Saxon bourgeois stereotype. At the same time the truly indigenous Americans, the Indians, were treated with a vileness, cruelty, and hypocrisy hardly equaled in the annals of civilization. The rich contributions to a United States culture that could have come from the Indians, and those that could have come from the masses of immigrant working people, have been almost wiped out. And along with this destruction of cultural sources that were especially rich in music, the predominant commercial culture has been notorious for its racist "humor," its sneering at and mockery of every real or fancied national characteristic brought to these shores.

The most obvious and destructive contradiction is that involving the Negro people. The Negro people have made the most vital contribution of any people to American music. This contribution was made always on the narrow, limited grounds permitted to the Negro people in a society in which they were segregated, given the hardest labor at the most meager pay, barred from most educational and professional opportunities and, in the states where the most Negroes live, from the vote and from civil rights of any kind. Occasional philanthropic grants were given to a handful. The stereotype was created that Negro music was supposed to be "crude," best when unlearned and "unconscious," fit only for song and dance entertainment for white audiences. Yet not only were great Tinpan Alley fortunes made on the material taken from the music of the Negro people, but a great mass of the serious composed music by white composers, when it tried to be most "American," showed the influence of the creative qualities of the music of the Negro people. Jim Crow is still the rule in music. Negro and white musicians sometimes play together in jazz bands, but in most bands segregation is enforced, and in all the highly paid "society" bands, Negroes cannot get a job. The opera companies and symphony orchestras are wholly lily-white, despite the existence of numbers of outstanding Negro singers and instrumentalists. A Negro may enter a northern school of music, although the fees are generally prohibitive, and may even win a scholarship. When he graduates, however, he cannot get any of the jobs which a white composer uses to make a living while he composes, such as writing for newspapers, teaching in the universities and schools, getting Hollywood or radio commissions. If an occasional Negro, by the most phenomenal talent and herculean effort, gets a prize award and some recognition in concert music and composition, he is under almost overhelming pressure to be submerged in the escapism and formalism that sets the standard for "serious" music. The false alternative appears between the stereotypes of the commercialized "popular" music and the cosmopolitanism of the "highbrow" art. There is no avenue through which a Negro composer can work directly for his own people, speaking directly and openly to them, for the poverty and Jim Crow enforced upon the Negro people make this impossible.

The repression of the music of the Negro people has a disastrous effect on all American music. This is seen in the flabbiness of the "popular" musical theater, in the formalism of the "art" music, and most of all in the division between "art" and "popular."

The impassable barrier between "popular" and "art" music, which exists to a greater extent in the United States than in any other country in the world, is not natural to music or to people. It is an artificiality. It serves to keep "popular" music, the music most available to people, in the straitjacket and censorship of the music-factory owners who control its production, and to make the "art" composer feel helpless, alienated from the public, able to speak only to a narrow group of fellow composers and critics. This barrier is also chauvinist. It serves most specifically as a means for distorting and repressing the music of the Negro people, who have made the greatest contribution to what is called "popular," while exploiting them economically and intellectually, and keeping "art" music almost wholly lily-white. Yet the musical achievement of the Negro people under the most adverse conditions has already proved that a music can be created in America of the highest esthetic quality and the most immediate appeal and vivid human imagery.

There can be no great realistic music in the United States until composers realize that music must be a medium for the reflection of life and the battle of ideas, until the artificial barrier between the "popular" and "classical" is broken down, and until the bonds which restrict the musical development of the American Negro people are broken. If this fight is not undertaken, then United States music will continue to live on the fringes of cultural life, debased by commercial straitjackets and censorship, moving from the illusion of one formalist or craft system to the next, existing anemically on the crumbs falling from a few wealthy patrons or corporation advertising budgets. If such a fight is undertaken, then all music will take on a new power, meaning, and importance in life to the American people. Works will come forth which will inspire the American people in their collective struggles for peaceful progress, express their solidarity with all other struggling peoples, and be a historic contribution to world culture.

GLOSSARY OF MUSICAL TERMS

ARIA: Beginning first as a song set within a larger vocal work such as a cantata or opera, the aria developed in the eighteenth century as an elaborate melodic and dramatic form for solo voice and orchestra, brilliantly written to show off the powers of the voice, and often repeating words of the text many times over for musical effect. An aria was generally preceded by a recitative, a word-by-word setting of text to music, which in its speech-like inflections and rhythms was part speech, part song.

ARIOSO: A vocal form with melodic phrases like those of an aria set in a free, declamatory continuity resembling the recitative.

ATONAL MUSIC, ATONALITY: *See Harmony.*

CADENZA: A florid section inserted just before the closing passages of a movement in an aria or an instrumental work (most often found in the concerto), in which the soloist exhibits his ingenuity and skill in manipulating the themes of the music. Early cadenzas were improvised at the performance.

CANTATA: A setting of text to music, employing solo voices, chorus, or both, with orchestra, ranging in scope from an extended aria to a large body of arias and choruses.

CHANSON: *See Song.*

CHORALE: The German Lutheran hymn, or a melody in hymn style.

CHACONNE: *See Counterpoint.*

CHAMBER MUSIC: Music for a small group of performers, few enough so that each can play an individual role. Composed at first for home, private, or amateur performance, chamber music in the nineteenth century came to be written for concert performance, and built according to the general principles of sonata form. It generally embodied more reflective and intimate emotional experiences than the big orchestral forms. The basic instrumental combinations of chamber music are the sonata for solo instrument with piano, and the string quartet of two violins, viola, and cello. Works of chamber music are generally described by the number of instruments they are written for, a trio being for three instruments, a quartet for four, a quintet for five, etc.

CHORD: Two or more notes sounded at the same time. *See Harmony.*

CHROMATIC: *See Mode, Scale, and Key.*

CODA: *See Sonata Form.*

CONCERTO: Originally a style of composition based on the concept of alternating heavy and light masses of sound. The concerto became in the late seventeenth and eighteenth centuries a major form for the development of

purely instrumental music. A concerto was generally in three or more movements contrasting in tempo; and a typical concerto movement was one in which
statements of the basic melodies or themes were made by the massed body of
the orchestra, alternating with ingenious, touching, and brilliant exercises on
these themes, as well as on their harmony and rhythms, by a solo instrument
or a group of them. The writing for the solo instruments was in improvisational
style and, as the concerto developed, was strongly influenced by the opera aria.
The concerto became a major form for the public appearance of the masterful
solo performer, and in the late eighteenth century the concerto for solo piano
or violin with orchestra became the leading concerto form. Nineteenth century
concertos, in which the style of the orchestral writing approached the symphony,
also reached a high point of display of the brilliant dynamic and technical
powers of the soloists.

CONSONANCE: *See Harmony.*

COUNTERPOINT, CONTRAPUNTAL: Counterpoint is polyphonic, or
"many-voiced" music, organized on harmonic principles. "Baroque" counterpoint of the seventeenth and eighteenth centuries was the art of composing for
two or more interweaving melodic lines, their relationship guided by a controlling concept of tonality. An important tool in the counterpoint of this
period was the "baroque bass," "thorough bass," or "continuo," sometimes also
called a "figured bass" when it was not wholly written out. This was a bass
melodic line controlling the harmonic movement of the entire composition,
against which the upper melodic lines moved in various harmonic and rhythmic
pulls and tensions. Major contrapuntal forms of this period were the trio-sonata;
dance forms such as the chaconne and passacaglia, constructed on a bass theme
or "ground" repeated over and over; the chorale-prelude, in which a counterpoint was woven about a chorale and above all the fugue.

DANCE, DANCE FORMS: Closely connected with song as a major source of
human imagery throughout the entire history of music, most dances are songs
in which one can follow the bodily movements of the dance itself in the accents
and rhythmic pattern of the music. The seventeenth and eighteenth centuries
saw a vast amount of composition in simple or elaborate dance form, inspired
by the ballets, or dance sections, of opera, which in turn gave birth to the
dance suite, or collection of dances written for instruments. Many operatic
arias, and choral and vocal movements in the works of Purcell, Bach, Handel,
and Gluck, are in dance rhythm. The dances used were developments of both
the court and the folk dances of the Middle Ages. Some of the most popular
were the gavotte, allemande, sarabande, gigue, minuet, siciliana, passepied.
Characteristic of many dance forms is a contrasting middle section called a trio.
The march is a development of dance. The nineteenth century saw a great
infusion of popular and national dance images in large-scale compositions, some
being the Austrian *ländler,* the Polish mazurka and polonaise, the Czech polka
and *furiant,* the Hungarian *czardas,* the Russian *hopak,* the Spanish *jota.*

DISSONANCE: *See Harmony.*

FANTASY, FANTASIA: One of the freer and more experimental forms of the
seventeenth and eighteenth centuries, proceeding apparently like an improvisation, in which the composers depicted highly introspective moods and in the

process investigated some of the more unusual chromatic colors and key changes of major-minor harmony. The fantasy-piece was much used in the nineteenth century to express deep yearning and unresolved emotional conflicts; it was kin in free-flowing style to the rhapsody.

FUGUE: A compact and intricate contrapuntal form, often written for instruments, but retaining the polyphonic vocal principle of separate melodic lines, called "voices," each keeping its comparative integrity throughout the composition. There may be three or more such "voices" in a fugue. A fugue begins with a theme, or "subject," on which each voice enters in turn, as if "imitating" the preceding one. Each voice follows the subject with a "countersubject." This opening, called the "exposition," introduces the main material and all the voices. Then comes a "development" in which there are many "episodes," introducing new material, playing the voices against each other in various combinations, transforming the themes rhythmically and harmonically, taking the music far from the opening key or tonality. Finally there is a "recapitulation" in which the opening theme is reaffirmed in its original form by all the voices, uniting in an assertion of the opening tonality. The fugue had its origin in popular vocal music in which one voice "imitated" another by following it with the same melody, some examples being the Italian *ricercare* and *canzone,* the French *chanson,* the English round.

HARMONY: In the most general sense, the organization of the notes used in a musical performance in definite relationships to one another, the most important being the affirmation of one note as the "tonic," or "home note," another as the "dominant" or alternate resting place. The two form a kind of axis about which the other notes used in the performance cluster with various effects of intonation and degrees of tension. With the development of polyphony or many-voiced music, harmony began to refer to the simultaneous merged tones, or chords, produced by the interweaving melodies. With the development of the major-minor system, and the use of key and key change, harmony became the study of such problems as the chords which affirmed the presence of the various keys; the relation of chords to each other; the way in which chords were used in the movement from key to key; the way in which chords added depth, mood, and color to melodies. However, harmony also retained its broader meaning of the organization of an entire musical composition about the principles of tonality, and the movement away from and back to the "home" key. Basic to tonal music is the concept of dissonance, or a set of notes aurally clashing and demanding further movement and consonance, which the ear accepts as being at rest.

Twentieth century atonal music, such as Schönberg's, is a development of major-minor music in which the key shifts so constantly, and there is so constant a use of chromatic notes, that key itself is abandoned. The relations between consonance and dissonance disappear, and there are only various degrees of dissonance or "tension." Since there are no binding relationships between notes, chords, and keys, and since musical form is based on such relationships, all form, even that of a simple song, must disappear, and in spite of the intricate combinations of tone patterns worked out by the composer on paper, the ear hears only an unorganized continuity of sounds. Twentieth century polytonal music, such as Stravinsky's, employs melodic lines and chords in two or more different keys at the same time, and also uses the various instrumental timbres as controlling factors in the chords. Here, too, the effect of key and key change is abandoned. The melodic phrases begin to resemble those of primitive music, with a mechanization not found in the primitive, and the incessant repetition of rhythmic figures begins to play an overwhelming part in musical form.

HOMOPHONY, HOMOPHONIC: *See Polyphony.*

LIBRETTO: *See Opera.*

MADRIGAL: A popular form of musical composition in sixteenth century Italy and England, consisting of a lyric poem set for a small group of voices, generally no more than five, each of which sang the same words but preserved its individuality of accent and phrasing.

MAJOR AND MINOR: *See Mode, Scale, and Key.*

MASS: The major musical form of Catholic Church ritual, and a development of primitive ritual drama, depicting through a series of traditional Latin prayers, the *Kyrie, Gloria, Credo, Sanctus,* and *Agnus Dei,* the crucifixion and resurrection of Christ. A special form of the mass is the Requiem Mass, a service for the dead.

MELODY: A series of notes following each other in time which, through differences in pitch, accent, time duration, are bound together into a unit, which has the ability to convey emotion and human imagery.

MODE, SCALE, AND KEY: Modal music is found in all periods when music was wholly or largely improvised. Modes in the most general sense were traditional melodies or melodic phrases, used as a basis for improvisation. They acquired great intricacy and standardization when connected with magic and religious rituals, each mode having a special magic significance. Scales are more generalized bases for creating and analyzing music than modes, and rose along with the greater place of the instrument in music. A scale may be called the notes used by a work of music arranged in orderly succession. Modern European music (since 1600) is based on what are known as the diatonic scales, called this because of their special arrangement of whole and half notes. The important difference between music based on mode and the modern music based on scale is in the ability of the latter to "modulate," or change key. A performance in modal style, with few exceptions, revolves about the same tonal center throughout. However, in the modern music based on scale and on the major-minor system, a scale may be built on any given note. The name of this note becomes the key of the music. Thus a scale built on C is in the key of C, which is the "tonic" note or tonal center. The scale may be major (proceeding through two whole steps and then a half step) or minor (proceeding through a whole step and then a half step). During the course of a composition, it is possible to shift all the melodies, chords, and musical material, from major to minor and from a scale based on one key to a scale based on another. This shift of key, called modulation, makes possible a far greater organization of musical tones into one usable body, and also a far greater psychological and emotional content, than was possible in the old modal music. The chromatic scale consists of all the half steps arranged in order. Since all the steps, or intervals, are the same, the chromatic scale has no tonal center, no axis, and is not really a scale. Chromatic effects—adding notes not found in the scales being used, but not calling for an actual change of key—are used to add color, piquancy, and special moods to major-minor music. Music is also called chromatic when it shifts key so constantly that key itself is evanescent.

MOTET: A contrapuntal form used by both Catholic and Protestant Church composers, setting for voices a prayer other than the traditional liturgy of the mass. Also a popular form in the Middle Ages in which a traditional liturgical melody was combined contrapuntally with secular, folk, and even ribald songs.

MOVEMENT: A composition, self-contained in form, which is a section of a larger composition, such as a symphony, concerto, or suite.

OPERA: Drama set to music. The words of the drama and the arias are called the "book," or "libretto." A tradition of drama with music has existed from the earliest times, including the Greek dramas and the folk plays of the Middle Ages. Composed opera, known as such, began about 1600 in Italy. It is one of the errors of music theorists to deny importance and meaning to the librettos of opera. The best composers of opera have always been deeply concerned with the librettos they set, and sought the most advanced dramatic style of their time. The main styles of opera are the Italian *opera seria* of the seventeenth and eighteenth centuries, based on a poetic mythological text, with many elaborate arias; French opera of the seventeenth and early eighteenth centuries, also based on revivals of poetic classic drama and using stately declamation and many ballet, or dance, sections; the various forms of comic opera, of the same centuries, such as the Italian *opera buffa,* the German *singspiel,* and English ballad opera, which contained spoken dialogue, much folk and popular song, a great deal of ad-libbing, buffoonery, and political satire. In nineteenth century France "grand" opera, a kind of flamboyant historical and costume pageantry, was developed. The real division that developed, however, was between the subjectivism of the Wagner operas, on the one hand, with their symbols taken from ancient myths and magic, and a symphonic or tone-poem approach to musical form, in which the vocal line tended to dwindle in importance; and, on the other hand, the nationally conscious and historically realist opera of such men as Verdi, Mussorgsky, and Tchaikovsky, in which voice and song remained dominant.

ORATORIO: A large-scale form for solo singers, chorus, and orchestra, drawing heavily on operatic methods and applying them to a Biblical or religious subject or story, without, however, using costume, scenery, and stage action.

OVERTURE: An instrumental composition acting as an introductory movement or "curtain raiser" to a musical work, most often an opera or an oratorio. The eighteenth century French and Italian overtures were elaborate musical forms that had a powerful influence on the rise of the orchestral symphony. The nineteenth century overture tended to be a kind of descriptive or dramatic fantasy, often using melodies from the body of the opera, and summarizing its dramatic conflict. It had a powerful influence on the tone poem and the symphonic poem.

PASSACAGLIA: *See Dance Forms.*

PITCH: The quality that a musical note has of sounding relatively "higher" or "lower," depending on the rate of vibration of its sound wave. A faster rate of vibration will sound higher.

POLYPHONY: "Many-voiced" music or music of two or more interweaving melodic lines. Polyphonic music is contrasted to homophonic music, which is music of a single melodic line, either alone or supported by chords. In actual practice, all homophonic music has some polyphonic character, and all polyphonic music has some "vertical," or chord character, which would make it partly homophonic.

POLYTONALITY, POLYTONAL MUSIC: *See Harmony.*

PROGRAM MUSIC: Music guided in its form by a story, scene painting, dramatic action, or philosophical idea, this material being known as its "program." While program music has existed as long as music itself, its esthetic qualities were widely questioned during the nineteenth century, on the ground that it was not "pure" music and depended on non-musical supports. The controversy was touched off by Liszt's symphonic poems and piano "tone poems." The truth is that no music is really "pure," and all musical form must depend for its meaning on its relation to real life and human actions. Program music has been as artistically successful as any other form (examples being Beethoven's dramatic overtures, Berlioz' "Harold in Italy," Schumann's "Carnival," Smetana's "My Homeland" cycle and quartet "From My Life," Tchaikovsky's "Romeo and Juliet"). The weakness that appears in bad program music is often the vagueness of the program, more unreal and incomprehensible than the music, and the tendency to disguise this emptiness with musical naturalism, or the depiction of the actual sounds of nature such as wind, waves, battle noises, bleating sheep, etc. Such naturalism, for all its occasional usefulness, is a low level of depiction of life in music.

RHYTHM: The reflection in music of body movement, ranging from the heartbeat and the movements of labor to the intricacies and cross-movements of dance. A musical rhythm has a fundamental beat regularly repeated, like a pulse beat, sometimes called the "meter," or measure. Within this, there are clusters of notes of various accents and time duration, which create secondary impulses and beats, uniting with and at the same time opposed to the fundamental beat and thus giving the music a feeling of life and forward movement.

RONDO: A dance form derived from the ancient ring or round dance, and, in the Middle Ages, also a dance poem. Its main characteristic is the regular reappearance of its opening theme, or melody, as a kind of refrain, while between these reappearances comes contrasting and varied material. The rondo became a favorite last-movement form for symphony, sonata, and concerto because its repetition of the opening melody and tonality, along with its dance-like character, gave the music a strong sense of affirmation of life.

SCALE: *See Mode, Scale, and Key.*

SCHERZO: Meaning literally a musical "joke," the scherzo became a favorite third-movement form to Beethoven and subsequent composers, replacing the more sedate eighteenth century minuet with trio. The scherzo, which also had

a contrasting middle section or trio, had a lusty folk-dance quality, and could
be as well a music of witty and sardonic rhythmic fantasy.

SONATA, SONATA FORM: Sonata originally meant music to be sounded on
instruments, in contrast to cantata, or music to be sung. Sonata early became
a catch-all term for instrumental music, much of which was a direct transfer of
vocal style to instruments. By the late seventeenth and early eighteenth centuries
the "trio sonata" became established, along with the concerto, as a major
form for the development of instrumental music. "Trio" in this connection
referred not to the number of instruments, but to the number of "parts" or
"voices." A trio sonata was written in terms of a middle melodic voice, a bass
line or "thorough bass," and an upper-voice contrapuntal decoration, or "obbli-
gato." Such sonatas had a number of movements, most often four, and the
particular style of each movement could be taken from fugue, aria, choral-
prelude, a concerto movement, or the many dance forms of the time.

   The kind of music now known as sonata form (the music itself appeared
long before the description) flowered in the latter half of the eighteenth
century. It is homophonic, the controlling element being the melody in the
upper voice, supported by harmonies, although it may have many passages in
counterpoint. It is built with melodies or themes of contrasting key, rhythm,
and emotional character, introduced at or near the beginning. It proceeds through
differing and contrasting rhythmic patterns. Thus it is a qualitative leap over
the instrumental forms dominated by vocal style or by the unbroken rhythms
of dance forms. It may be described as instrumental music which embodies a
dramatic life in its very form and texture. Like the fugue, its structure is based
on harmonic movement away from and back to an opening tonality. It has an
exposition section, in which its main tonality is affirmed and material introduced;
a development section, in which there is a free rhythmic and harmonic transformation of the material; a recapitulation section, or return of the original
material and tonality; a coda, or second development, rounding out the movement,
sometimes very short and sometimes becoming a major section of the movement.
While works in sonata form have more than one movement, generally three or
four, it is the first movement which is tightest and most dramatic, and so
sonata form is sometimes called first-movement form. All the movements, however, are based in one way or another on the harmonic and rhythmic development of themes. While "sonata form" can refer to the symphony or music of
any instrumental combination, the term "sonata" now refers to a work in this
form written for a single instrument, such as a piano, or a combination of
two, such as violin and piano.

SONG: Song in primitive life took its name, content, and form from the
rituals and dances to which it was set. It was frequently "antiphonal"—that is,
built on the interplay of a leader's voice against a response by the people. Song
in the Middle Ages took its form from the intricacies of lyric poetry and from
dance. The growing secularization of composed music produced many forms of
song for groups of singers, examples being the French *chanson,* Italian *canzone*
and *villanella,* and finally the rich Italian and English madrigal. The late sixteenth and the seventeenth centuries produced the composed solo song with instrumental accompaniment, and at this time song took on a marked harmonic
construction, with the beginning and end strongly affirming the tonality and

the middle contrasting in key. Throughout its history, composed song delved into folk song for its material. Song became, in addition to a form in itself, a unit of human imagery which could enter into and lend its character to larger musical works, such as opera, cantata, sonata, symphony, concerto, etc. Song exhibits perfectly the basic character of music, so incomprehensible to many theorists. It has a form of its own and is at the same time a reflection of life. Thus the innumerable successful songs, folk and "art," follow the inflections of speech, bring out the character and emphasis of words, and at the same time intensify the emotions of the entire poem in the repetitions, variations, and rounded-out pattern of the melody.

SYMPHONY: Rising out of the "sinfonia," which was an instrumental overture to a vocal work, the symphony developed in the late eighteenth century and flowered in the early nineteenth century as a work in sonata form for full orchestra, the orchestra being treated as a great collective instrument capable of many colors and effects of loudness and softness. The symphony is generally in four movements. The first is most dramatic and representative of conflict. The second is generally slow and reflective, with the character of an extended and developed song. The third is generally a dance with trio, or a scherzo. It is the last movement which has assumed the greatest variety of forms. This arises from the fact that the symphony itself, through the circumstances under which it developed, became essentially a means for the public expression of profound social and philosophical views. Thus the last movement had to embody a summation and resolution. This problem also arose in the solo sonata, chamber music, and the concerto. Some of the forms taken by closing movements are a rondo (often with a development section resembling sonata form), a choral cantata (as in Beethoven's Ninth Symphony), a fugue, a passacaglia, a theme and variations. Sometimes, carrying out more obviously this character of a summation, there is a quotation of material from the earlier movements.

SYMPHONIC POEM, TONE POEM: *See Program Music.*

TEMPO: Tempo refers to the rate of movement of a musical work, generally signified by traditional Italian words such as (proceeding from the slowest to the fastest) largo, adagio, andante, allegro, presto.

TONALITY: *See Harmony; also Mode, Scale and Key.*

THEME: A theme is a musical phrase used as a unit in a larger musical construction. A theme may be a melody; a fully rounded song or dance with a beginning, middle, and end; or a short phrase of a few notes. In the last case, its virtue is its ability to be used for a continuous series of extended and complicated harmonic manipulations.

TIMBRE: The "tone color" of a human voice or a musical instrument. This "color" comes from the presence in a musical tone not only of a main wave vibration setting its pitch, but also of accompanying lesser and partial vibrations, which are called "overtones." Each instrumental timbre has its own characteristic pattern of overtones.

TONALITY: *See Harmony; also Mode, Scale, and Key.*

REFERENCE NOTES

CHAPTER TWO

1. Henri Prunières, *A New History of Music,* p. 7, N. Y., 1943.
2. J. Huizinga, *The Waning Middle Ages,* p. 31, London, 1937.
3. Prunières, *op. cit.,* p. 23.
4. Curt Sachs, *Our Musical Heritage,* p. 101, N. Y., 1948.
5. Prunières, *op. cit.,* p. 40.
6. Paul Henry Lang, *Music in Western Civilization,* p. 110, N. Y., 1941.
7. *Ibid.,* p. 166.
8. Ernst Meyer, *English Chamber Music,* p. 33, London, 1946.
9. Lang, *op. cit.,* p. 127.
10. Frederick Engels, *Ludwig Feuerbach,* p. 57, N. Y., 1941.
11. Curt Sachs, *The Commonwealth of Art,* p. 87, N. Y., 1946.
12. *Ibid.,* p. 122.

CHAPTER THREE

1. Hans T. David and Arthur Mendel, eds., *The Bach Reader,* p. 49, N. Y., 1946.
2. *Ibid.,* pp. 238-47.
3. Karl Marx and Frederick Engels, *Literature and Art,* p. 20, N. Y., 1947.
4. *The Bach Reader,* p. 279.
5. Emily Anderson, ed., *The Letters of Mozart and His Family,* Vol. 3, p. 1097, London, 1938.
6. Alfred Einstein, *Mozart,* p. 433, N. Y., 1945.
7. *The Letters of Mozart and His Family,* Vol. 3, p. 1381.
8. *Ibid.,* p. 1407.

CHAPTER FOUR

1. V. G. Belinsky, *Selected Philosophical Works,* p. 214, Moscow, 1948.
2. A. Schindler, *Life of Beethoven,* p. 315, Boston.
3. *Ibid.,* p. 31.
4. *Ibid.,* p. 35.
5. *Ibid.,* p. v.
6. Otto Erich Deutsch, *A Schubert Reader,* p. 284, N. Y., 1947.

CHAPTER FIVE

1. Deutsch, *op. cit.,* p. 136.
2. *Ibid.,* p. 149.

3. Schindler, *op. cit.*, pp. 144-46.
4. Hector Berlioz, *Memoirs*, p. 142, N. Y., 1932.
5. *Ibid.*, p. 103.
6. *Ibid.*, p. 217.
7. *Ibid.*, p. xi.

CHAPTER SIX

1. Introduction by Frederick Engels to Karl Marx, *The Class Struggles in France*, p. 13, N. Y., n.d.

CHAPTER SEVEN

1. Franz Werfel and Paul Stefan, *Verdi: The Man in His Letters*, p. 290, N. Y., 1942.
2. *Ibid.*, p. 360.
3. Lyof N. Tolstoi, *What Is to Be Done?*, p. 213, N. Y., 1925.

CHAPTER EIGHT

1. Dika Newlin, *Bruckner, Mahler, Schoenberg*, p. 253, N. Y., 1947.
2. V. I. Lenin, "The Tasks of the Youth Leagues," *The Young Generation*, p. 31, N. Y., 1940.
3. Notes to Igor Stravinsky, *Les Noces*, Columbia Records, Album No. 204.
4. "Stravinsky and the Theatre," *Dance Index*, Vol. VI, Nos. 10, 11, 12, 1947, pp. 276-77.
5. *Modern Music*, May-June 1934, p. 169.
6. Eric W. White, *Stravinsky*, p. 92, N. Y., 1948.
7. *Ibid.*, p. 93.
8. Notes to Igor Stravinsky, *Symphony in Three Movements*, Columbia Records, Album No. 680.

CHAPTER NINE

1. *Speaking of Peace: Reports Delivered at the Cultural and Scientific Conference for World Peace, March 25-27, 1949*, pp. 98-99, National Council of the Arts, Sciences, and Professions, N. Y., 1949.
2. Andrei A. Zhdanov, *Essays on Literature, Philosophy, and Music*, p. 92, N. Y., 1950.
3. *Ibid.*, p. 78.
4. *Ibid.*, p. 86.
5. *Journal of the American Musicological Society*, Fall 1950, pp. 236-55.

CHAPTER TEN

1. *New York Times Book Review*, Dec. 31, 1950, p. 6.